MASTERING
STAND-UP

MASTERING STAND-UP

THE COMPLETE GUIDE TO BECOMING A SUCCESSFUL COMEDIAN

Stephen Rosenfield

CHICAGO
REVIEW
PRESS

Published by Chicago Review Press Incorporated
814 North Franklin Street
Chicago, Illinois 60610
ISBN 978-1-61373-692-0

Library of Congress Cataloging-in-Publication Data
Is available from the Library of Congress.

Cover design: John Yates at Stealworks
Cover image: Getty Images / Espen Dalmo (www.8thsession.com)
Typesetting: Nord Compo

Printed in the United States of America
5 4 3 2 1

To the snake in the Garden of Eden. Without this snake, humankind would lack the two absolute essentials of comedy: problems and knowledge. Adam and Eve were happy before the snake arrived and that's nice, but happiness is not funny. The laughs start when the problems start and we have knowledge of them. It's the snake that created the circumstances for laughter on Earth.

CONTENTS

PREFACE

THE STAND-UP COMEDY EXPERIENCE STARTED FOR ME in my living room on East 58th Street in Manhattan. I was a director and writer in the theater then. One day a stand-up named Eli Krupnick came to my apartment and said he wanted to work with me. I'd worked with dozens of actors to build strong, memorable performances. In my first off-Broadway show, a sketch comedy show that I directed and coauthored, our lead, Lee Wilkof, won the Obie Award for acting. In Los Angeles I had directed the revival of the Charles Strouse musical *Charlie and Algernon*, and our star, P. J. Benjamin, won the L.A. Weekly and Drama-Logue Awards. I had ventured into the comedy club scene with a sketch comedy group that I directed and wrote for, Rubber Feet, who became regulars at the Comic Strip. But I'd never worked with a stand-up before.

I was excited by the idea, though. For as long as I can remember, I have loved stand-up comedy. Stand-ups were the reason I watched *The Ed Sullivan Show*. I skipped a day of high school to see Lenny Bruce perform in the East Village.

Eli and I started to work together, and after hearing of our success, other new stand-ups began arriving at my door. None of them had training as actors. So we worked together on identifying what emotions underpinned their jokes and how to play those emotions on a comedy club stage. If a joke felt weak, we would rewrite it together.

I noticed that shortening the setup and the punch, making a joke less generic and more personal, and shaping jokes to fit the persona of the comedian would bring new vitality to their performances. Our work together paid off. It's easy to determine that in stand-up comedy. You get more laughs and more gigs, and you start getting paid.

Eventually Eli suggested I conduct a workshop. Ten students met with me as a class twice a week for three weeks. Additionally, I met with them individually to work on their writing. In class they tested out their material and acted as an audience for each other. After their class presentation, they received detailed feedback from me. The workshop culminated in a performance at Don't Tell Mama, the legendary cabaret on West 46th Street. Afterward I gave them notes on their performance.

At that point, there was only one other stand-up workshop in New York, and no one in the city had developed a program that would give comics the opportunity to receive instruction straight through the whole process, from writing new jokes to performing them at a club. This first workshop took place in November 1988. It was the birth of the American Comedy Institute, a comedy school for performers and writers that now draws students from all across America and around the world.

I had come to stand-up from the world of the theater, where creating entertainment takes significant amounts of time, money, and people. The results can be magical, provocative, and breathtaking. But as I began to immerse myself in the world of stand-up, I saw that one person on an empty stage could serve up equally compelling entertainment. Theater, film, and television are all technologically sophisticated mediums employed, essentially, to tell a story. Stand-ups do the same thing, but their only technological need is, if the room is big, a microphone. This fact gives stand-ups the ability to create entertainment about the present moment—now. What happened today, in the world and in their lives. The theater can do many things magnificently, but it can't do that. Increasingly for me, a comedy club was the place I could regularly go for terrific entertainment that related to me and the moment I was living in.

The first stand-ups I worked with came from all walks of life. What they had in common was a sense of humor, a desire to be onstage, and the urgent need to communicate through comedy. Through my work with them I discovered that I had a gift for helping transform funny people into comedians.

And oh, what people! Olga Namer is a young woman who was raised in an Orthodox Jewish community in Brooklyn. Her community did its utmost to shelter its children from the world beyond their religious beliefs and cultural traditions. Her family's expectation was that she would lead her life within the confines of their neighborhood. But there was a problem. Olga is funny. Very, very funny. And when someone has a powerful comic voice inside them, that comic voice pushes hard to get out. Olga came to study with me, and now she does stand-up about her struggles to break free of her upbringing and live in the secular world.

A young man named Joseph Opio came to work with me from Uganda, where he had produced, written, and performed in a TV show modeled after *The Daily Show with Jon Stewart*. Now he's a staff writer on *The Daily Show with Trevor Noah*.

A particularly dedicated student was a young man who had a well-paying job at Gray Advertising, but who had absolutely made up his mind to leave corporate life and become a stand-up. His name is Jim Gaffigan. A high school sophomore from Brooklyn came to study with me. At 16 she was writing stand-up material that was original, personal, smart, sexy, and funny. That was Lena Dunham. Zinat Pirzadeh—a stand-up who was raised in Iran and fled to Sweden—came to America to study with me. She told me that she'd received death threats from extremists in Swedish Muslim communities and from neo-Nazis. Fearing for her life, she had given up stand-up for two years. Longing to get back onstage, she faced a decision: she could allow herself to be bullied into silence for the rest of her life, or she could continue to pursue her comedy despite the dangers. She returned to the stage. Zinat risked her life to perform stand-up comedy. She is now one of Sweden's leading comedians.

The stories continue and each is unique, and it has been a joy working with these talented people and seeing them grow.

I've been moving people forward in their comedy careers for 28 years. I've written this book because I would enjoy doing the same for you.

The book is divided into five parts. The first part contains advice I share with comedians at the outset of our working together. The second part is devoted to all the forms that stand-up comedy can take. Knowing these forms will expand your understanding of how to express yourself as a comedian. The third part is a handbook for creating stand-up comedy material. Here you will learn how to write stand-up jokes that are original, tightly written, and funny. The fourth part is the handbook for performing stand-up comedy. This part will help you become a vivid, likable, and memorable performer. The fifth part of the book is called "Get Undeniably Good." This part deals with how to successfully engage in the ongoing journey to master the art and crafts of stand-up.

If this is the journey you want to take, turn the page.

Part I

BEGINNING OUR WORK TOGETHER

1

THINGS I KNOW ABOUT YOU

YOU HAVE A LOT OF COMEDY INSIDE YOU. I don't want you to ever doubt that fact again. There are only a few things I know absolutely; this is one of them. You may ask yourself, *How the hell can he say that? He doesn't know me. He's not even here.* Here's how I know. Would you have picked up this book if you didn't have a sense of humor? Put your palm out so I can read it. All your life people have told you how funny you are. Sometimes you didn't even think you were being funny, but people laughed. If someone other than you was the class clown in school, you heard what that person put out there for laughs, and thought to yourself, *I'm funnier.* You were right. And the people who've been telling you that you're funny, they're right too.

So now, knowing you, you're probably thinking, *OK, I'm funny with my friends and family, but that doesn't mean I could be funny onstage or write comedy professionally.* You're wrong again. I'm sorry to keep contradicting you, but I feel I owe you the truth. You've been nice enough to pick up my book. There are tons of other books you could be reading right now, but you've picked mine. So now we have a relationship. And when a relationship is founded on comedy, there has to be absolute candor. Why? Because the truth comes out quickly in comedy. It comes out the moment you get in front of an audience. Either they laugh or they don't. If I insincerely tell you that you're funny, and you believe me and go out in front of an audience and get no laughs, then you won't believe me again—and that will be the end of our relationship. I have to be honest with you because I know the audience is going to be honest with you.

Here's the truth: if you're funny with your friends and family, that's a sign you'll be funny onstage and that you can be both a writer and a performer of comedy. You have the talent. What you need now is the craft. Craft is what will transform your comedy from an entertainment for friends and family to an entertainment for a mass national audience. I can teach you the craft of performing and writing comedy. It's an exciting thought—you, onstage at a comedy club, getting big laughs; you, submitting your comedy writing to a television show and hearing back about a staff writer position.

It's exciting, but let's not uncork the champagne yet. You have to get very, very good at stand-up for good things to happen. And I don't mean good once in a while, when you give a terrific performance. I mean good night after night after night after night; in small clubs and in big clubs; in your town and in towns and cities across the country; in front of packed audiences and sparse audiences; in front of people who know you and like you, and in front of complete strangers; in front of great audiences and dead audiences; opening a show and closing a show; following a comic who bombs and following a comic who kills; when you're pumped and when you feel like crap; when . . . you get the idea.

When you get this good, undeniably good, you'll have a career as a stand-up comedian. I guarantee it. There's no such thing as a great undiscovered comedian. There are "table comics," stand-ups who are hilarious at the comics' table while having a drink after the show but not hilarious when and where it counts: showtime onstage. When you consistently get big laughs on stage from the beginning to the end of your set with original, tightly written material, the people who hire comedians will hear those laughs and hire you. Guaranteed.

What does it take to get undeniably good? Talent, yes, but mostly work. Lots of work. Years of work. Great talents are people who are *obsessed* with their work. Are you up for this?

Don't answer yet. There is something else you need to know before you make this decision. You don't *need* to put in all this work. There are legions of generic comics getting laughs with jokes that anyone can tell, giving performances that are sometimes funny but never indelible. You see these people all the time at open mics, at "new talent nights," at regular shows, even on television. If you're OK with being one of them, don't be ashamed. It will save you a lot of time. And some money—you don't need to buy my book. I am not the right guy for you. We wouldn't be happy with each other and neither of us wants to get involved in something that's not going to work out. The only thing I ask is, if you're reading this book in a store, please put it back carefully. If you tear the cover or get a smudge on the page, it's harder to sell. Let's part as friends.

If, however, you're interested in creating original comedy—if you're excited about using your life, your experiences, your opinions, your observations, and your imagination to create comedy that the world will know is yours and yours alone—then uncork that bottle, sweetheart, and let's get cookin'. Cheers!

2

THE ROAD AHEAD

SUCCESSFUL COMEDIANS GET GOOD AT 12 THINGS. Get undeniably good at each of these and you can kiss your day job good-bye. You will be a pro. Here is the stand-up comedian's to-do list:

1. **Find Your Originality.** Get in touch with what is original about your sense of humor. Originality is a hallmark of exceptional art. In comedy, it's what the entertainment industry looks for first and foremost when determining who has the makings for the big leagues. Most club comics aren't originals. Their work is generic. Their material may get laughs, but it could be performed by anybody. That's why they're not memorable. And then, on the other hand, there are the stars of comedy. They make an indelible impression on us. We feel like we know them. We think of them as friends, as family. We love them. When they finish a set, the buzz in the room is not about jokes, it's about them. I'm going to help make that happen for you.

2. **Master the Techniques of Stand-Up Comedy Writing.** You may not think of yourself as a writer. You may think of yourself as just a funny person who says funny things. The idea of trying to write comedy may be intimidating. But it shouldn't

6

be, for one simple reason: you're already writing comedy. Like many comedy writers, you're writing with your mouth. What you need to do now is capture the funny things you say and think by writing them down. Once you get your spontaneous comic creations on paper, you can start to apply the writing techniques that will transform your ad-libs into stage-worthy stand-up comedy material.

3. **Master the Techniques of Stand-Up Comedy Performing.** Sometimes new comics feel like if they know their lines, they're prepared to do their set. Not true. That would be like an actor saying he doesn't need any rehearsal because he's memorized his lines. A stand-up, like an actor, must have the ability to produce onstage the emotions that give life to his performance. He must be capable of creating this emotional life night after night, in a way that seems spontaneous and unrehearsed to the audience. Masterful comedians acquire the techniques to do this, and it's the reason why many of them become exceptional actors. In the upcoming chapters, you'll learn how to acquire these skills.

4. **Create Your Comic Persona.** To become a successful comedian, you must develop a vivid and distinctive onstage personality—a personality as individual as your real-life personality, only more so. This stage personality, or *persona* as it's called in comedy, must be manifest in your material, how you look, what you wear, and how you move and speak. The process of creating a persona is a collaboration between you and your audiences over an extended period of time, usually several years. I'll teach you how to make this collaboration happen successfully.

5. **Deepen Your Understanding of Comedy.** Gifted stand-ups go on to careers as actors, writers, directors, and producers in television, theater, and movies; as hosts of their own television talk shows; and as bestselling authors. Their versatility comes from the knowledge and experience they acquire about comedy during their formative years in stand-up. Getting good

at stand-up writing and performing is an education that will enable you to pursue comedy in all areas of the arts and entertainment.

6. **Study Great Comedians.** Watching great comedians will help you learn and improve your act. Just because someone is onstage doing stand-up doesn't mean that you should study that person and try to incorporate what they're doing into your work. The comedians you love are the comedians you want to study. Louis C.K. says that studying George Carlin taught him what he needed to know to move up in the stand-up ranks from hack to comedy star. Carlin's work taught Louis the two things that became Louis's trademark. The first is to have the courage to speak the unspeakable onstage. And the second is that if, every year, you throw out all your old material and write an hour of new material, you will be forced to dig deeper and deeper into yourself to find your comedy. Don't limit yourself to studying only the current crop of star stand-ups. View video of the great stand-ups of the past. The Internet has made this easy. You're not going to know what's possible to accomplish in your stand-up unless you know the work of the great comedians who came before you.

7. **Perform! Perform! Perform!** To become a pro, performing must be a regular part of your workweek. Perform stand-up as frequently as you can. The only way you'll absorb the techniques you learn from this book is to use them onstage over and over again until they've become second nature to you.

8. **Never Blame Your Audience.** Your audience can be an invaluable guide to improving your writing and performing. In comedy, they're ultimately your editor in chief. Over time, they'll teach you what subjects and attitudes work best for you. Just as important, they'll teach you what doesn't work for you. Sometimes they'll be your friends and sometimes they'll be strangers; sometimes they'll love you and sometimes they'll be cold and indifferent; sometimes they'll be rude and sometimes you'll wish you could take them home with you because they'll

give you more than anyone else in the world gives you. They'll do all of these things, some of the time. Remember, however, that all of the time, they're your collaborators. In good shows and bad, they have lessons to teach you about how to be a better comedian. Never blame an audience; learn from them, instead. This book will teach you how.

9. **Know the Forms of Stand-Up Comedy.** As in all art, stand-up has classical forms. Knowing them will help you define and clarify the type of stand-up you want to do. Knowledge of the forms will expand and give shape to your comic ideas.

10. **Understand the Business.** To work as a stand-up, you need to be knowledgeable about the comedy business. There have never been more opportunities for comedians and comedy writers than there are now. Because of the Internet, it's possible for you to create and produce, at virtually no cost, comedy that can launch you professionally. I intend for you not only to do stand-up, but also to be *paid* to do stand-up. I'll provide you with a working knowledge of the entertainment industry.

11. **Trust Your Nerves.** It's OK to be nervous. Your nerves can give you invaluable assistance onstage. In this book, you'll learn how to make your nerves work for you.

12. **Have Fun.** Stand-up is the one endeavor I know of where having fun is actually a requirement. And it's a requirement for this reason: when individuals become an audience, a transformation takes place. They stop feeling what each of them is feeling individually, and they start to feel collectively what the performer is feeling. If the audience picks up from you that there's nowhere else on Earth you'd rather be than onstage talking to them, then they start thinking, *I'm having a ball here, listening to this guy.* If, however, you go onstage thinking, *Christ, let me get this over with*, then your audience will start thinking, *GET THIS OVER WITH.* Before each of our shows, I ask the comedians, "What's the most important thing tonight?" The answer is, have fun.

Now that you know what you're working toward, we're ready to begin. Remember this moment. The memory will make you smile when you're standing in the wings, waiting to go on for your first television special.

3

"NO!"

BENJAMIN FRANKLIN SAID, "In this world nothing can be said to be certain, except death and taxes." He was wrong. There's one other thing that's for certain. When people discover that you're doing stand-up, someone undoubtedly will say, "Oh, you're a comedian! Tell me a joke!" This chapter explains why you should say "No!"

First, let's examine what they're asking. They want you to tell them something funny that they can later retell to other people and get laughs. This is material like, "A priest, a rabbi, and a nun are in a lifeboat . . ." Or "A man walks into a bar with a kangaroo . . ." Or "How many strippers does it take to screw in a lightbulb?" That kind of joke is a riddle or a short story with a cast of characters and one laugh line at the end.

You're going to say "No!" because stand-ups don't use this joke form. They did in the past. Watch video of Myron Cohen and you'll see a famous comedian of the 1950s whose act involved telling these kinds of jokes. You can find his work on the Internet. He was a joke-teller who often used an Old World Jewish accent when he acted out characters. He was a big star—and funny. Watch him and you will laugh. You will also see why comedians haven't used this form since the 1960s.

Myron could take two minutes before he got to a laugh line. Jokes of this kind can take that amount of time or longer to get

11

to a laugh. If we're on a break at work, or at a gathering of family and friends, taking that much time to deliver a laugh is fine. It's not fine, however, in a comedy club. Because comedy club audiences have watched late-night TV comedians for years, they've been trained to expect laughs far more frequently. Watch the opening monologues of former *Tonight Show* hosts Johnny Carson and Jay Leno. Watch Jimmy Kimmel's, Stephen Colbert's, and Jimmy Fallon's monologues. These late-night comedians get upward of four laughs per minute. Watch video of David Letterman performing his Top Ten Lists. He can get laughs every five seconds. These laughs-per-minute ratios are what's expected of a stand-up. Riddle jokes and short story jokes with one laugh line at the end don't deliver laughs nearly that frequently. One reason stand-ups don't tell these kinds of jokes is that they take much too long to get a laugh.

To explain the second reason they don't tell them, I want to share one of my favorite Myron Cohen jokes. It's been a long time since I watched him tell it, so I'm doing it from memory:

> This man is not feeling so good at work and decides to come home early. It's two in the afternoon. When he gets home he calls out, "Honey, I'm home!" and there is no answer. He goes up to their bedroom to see if everything is all right and he sees his wife naked in bed. He looks at her and asks, "What's going on?" She says, "Nothing." The husband opens up his closet and there is a naked man standing there. "What are you doing here?!" he demands. The naked man replies, "Everybody's got to be someplace."

Myron Cohen told this joke and got laughs, I tell this joke and get laughs, and you can too—anyone can. A joke that anyone can tell and get laughs with is the definition of a generic joke. You don't want those in your act. You want jokes that are so clearly stamped with your personality, your opinions, and your attitudes that no one can tell them as successfully as you. That's the kind of comedy material that makes you pop out as an original and moves you up in the stand-up comedy ranks.

People don't go to comedy clubs to hear material that they've heard other people tell, or even worse, told themselves. A study revealed that a joke travels our entire country within 72 hours. Given all our social media, this makes sense. It's fair to assume that if you've heard a joke, so have a lot of other people—and some of those people may be in your audience. Yet another reason for the "No."

You're going to say "No" to people who ask you for a joke because if you're doing it right, you won't have the kind of joke they're looking for. Your set will be composed of original jokes that are imbued with your persona, your point of view. These jokes will be carefully ordered so that there's a flow: one joke contributes to the next; one joke is woven into the next joke to form a brilliant tapestry of comedy. You can't just pull out a thread for the "tell me a joke" guy. He probably won't get it without experiencing it in the context of your whole set. It would be like someone saying to a songwriter, "Oh, you write music! Sing me a note!" "No!" Tell him that you'd love for him to hear *all* of your jokes—and give him the time, place, and cover charge for your next performance.

The chapters in the next part of this book will introduce you to the contemporary forms of stand-up comedy.

Part II

THE FORMS OF STAND-UP COMEDY

4

OBSERVATIONAL STAND-UP

IN ALL ART, INCLUDING STAND-UP COMEDY, there is form and there is content. They are two different things. Form refers to a structure. Content refers to what is inside that structure. Observational stand-up refers to a writing structure designed to express the comedian's observations, opinions, and feelings about what's going on around him or her. This structure can house content about various things: the news, politics, pop culture, your life, and so on. It's a structure of stand-up writing that you can employ to create jokes about anything that crosses your comedic mind.

Observational stand-up jokes are unlike funny stories, which have a beginning, middle, and end. An observational joke can be one sentence long, like this Jay Leno joke:

If God wanted us to vote, he would give us candidates.

An observational stand-up piece can be any length. What distinguishes it as observational is that there is no story. There are only observations. Here's an excerpt from an extended observational piece by Johnny Carson:

Democracy is buying a big house you can't afford, with money you don't have, to impress people you wish were dead. And, unlike communism, democracy does not mean having just one ineffective political party; it means having two ineffective political parties. . . . Democracy is welcoming people from other lands, and giving them something to hold on to—usually a mop or a leaf blower. . . . And finally democracy is the eagle on the back of a dollar bill, with thirteen arrows in one claw, thirteen leaves on a branch, thirteen tail feathers, and thirteen stars over its head—this signifies that when the white man came to this country, it was bad luck for the Indians, bad luck for the trees, bad luck for the wildlife, and lights out for the American eagle.

Leno and Carson were longtime hosts of *The Tonight Show*, and both were rightfully famous for their opening monologues. Their monologues were composed mostly of observational stand-up jokes. To this day observational stand-up is the go-to form for jokes about the news. These jokes are short, they can be written quickly, and audiences delight in hearing funny things about what just happened today.

They also delight in hearing funny things about the age they live in. Many of the leading comedians of the 1960s and '70s—comedians like Lenny Bruce, Mort Sahl, Dick Gregory, George Carlin, Richard Pryor, Jackie "Moms" Mabley—reflected their tumultuous times by creating observational jokes about racism, violence, social and political upheaval, and religious and social hypocrisy. For example:

I won't say ours was a tough school, but we had our own coroner.

—Lenny Bruce

When you're born you get a ticket to the freak show; when you're born in America, you get a front-row seat.

—George Carlin

I woke up in an ambulance. And it wasn't nothing but white people staring at me. I said, "Ain't this a bitch. I done died and wound up in the wrong muthafucking heaven."

—Richard Pryor

Anytime you see me with my arms around an old man, I'm holding him for the police.

—Jackie "Moms" Mabley

The comedian considered to be the king of observational comedy is Jerry Seinfeld. His formative years as a stand-up were the 1980s. With a popular president (Reagan), no Vietnam War, and no Watergate scandal, the countercultural movement quieted down. Seinfeld, through his observational stand-up, refocused stand-up comedy's gaze from the big issues to the smallest of issues—the absurdity of things in our everyday lives that we accept and take for granted:

Now they show you how detergents take out bloodstains, a pretty violent image there. I think if you've got a T-shirt with a bloodstain all over it, maybe laundry isn't your biggest problem. Maybe you should get rid of the body before you do the wash.

I was the best man at a wedding. . . . If I'm the best man, why is she marrying him?

The Swiss have an interesting army. Five hundred years without a war. Pretty impressive. Also pretty lucky for them. Ever see that little Swiss Army knife they have to fight with? Not much of a weapon there. Corkscrews. Bottle openers. "Come on, buddy, let's go. You get past me, the guy in back of me, he's got a spoon. Back off. I've got the toe-clippers right here."

Observational stand-up is a wonderfully vital and adaptable form of comedy. It has been employed by generations of comedians to give shape to their comic ideas about big issues, small issues, issues we experience at a comfortable distance, and issues that are the most intimate and urgent matters of life. This brings us to the observational stand-up of Tig Notaro.

In less than a year Notaro went from being a respected but little-known comedian to a comedy sensation as a result of a breakout set she performed after she was diagnosed with breast cancer. Here is an observational piece drawn from this historic set she performed on *Conan*:

> Here's a little tidbit about me. I was diagnosed with bilateral breast cancer. And I ended up getting a double mastectomy. And before I had a double mastectomy I was already pretty flat chested. And I made so many jokes over the years about how small my chest was that I started to think that maybe my boobs overheard me. And were just like, "You know what? We're sick of this. Let's kill her."

Before I end this chapter, I want to share with you some observational stand-up written by my favorite comedian. He's the funniest and most profound stand-up I've ever encountered. I'm not going to tell you who he is before you read a few of his jokes. See if you can guess:

> Suppose you were an idiot. And suppose you were a member of Congress. But I repeat myself.
>
> God created war so that Americans would learn geography.
>
> What would men be without women? Scarce, mighty scarce.
>
> I've lived through some terrible things in my life, some of which actually happened.
>
> Giving up smoking is the easiest thing in the world. I know because I've done it thousands of times.

Those fresh and funny jokes were written by Mark Twain about 125 years ago. As the author of *Tom Sawyer* and *The Adventures of Huckleberry Finn*, Twain is revered as one of our greatest writers. What is less well known about him is that he toured the country giving lectures that were, essentially, stand-up comedy performances. Mark Twain *created* observational stand-up. Many great comedians have followed in his footsteps but, for me, none have surpassed him.

Here are some important things I've observed about Twain's writing:

- His writing is conversational. It's meant to be spoken, not read. Writing like this creates the illusion that the comedian is ad-libbing, talking off the top of his head, when in reality he's delivering carefully crafted, written jokes. The biggest laughs come when the audience thinks you're making it up on the spot.
- His writing is tight. The jokes are set up and delivered in one or two short sentences. ("Brevity is the soul of wit." —Shakespeare. "He's right." —Rosenfield)
- He doesn't lecture his audience. He talks to them about things they already know. What is surprising, original, and funny is his take on these things.
- There is a vivid and distinctive voice to his writing. His comic persona is embedded in his writing. It all sounds like it's coming from him and only him.
- His jokes get laughs—not smiles, not giggles, but laughs, big juicy laughs. He doesn't settle for less.
- After 125 years, his jokes are still funny. It's a safe bet that 125 years from now people won't laugh at jokes about Monica Lewinsky, Janet Reno, Dan Quayle, Michael Jackson, Elizabeth Taylor, Dick Cheney, Bill Clinton, or Donald Trump. There are names on this list that already mean nothing to many people. Yet in their day they were subjects of countless successful jokes. At the time, they made people laugh—mission accomplished for stand-ups. If, however, you can create comedy about the deepest things, the things we all share, men and women both, the things that matter and are true from one generation to the next, your jokes, like Mark Twain's, will have a very, very long shelf-life.

From the 19th century till today, comedians have employed observational stand-up to create comedy about their lives, comedy about their times, and comedy for the ages. When a form of stand-up comedy has this longevity, use it.

5

ANECDOTAL STAND-UP

A PREHISTORIC PERSON TELLING A STORY around the fire was probably the beginning of stand-up comedy.

It must have gone something like this: Ancient tribesmen were sent out on a hunting expedition. When they returned, they regaled the tribe with stories of their exploits. One of the hunters strove to give an entirely accurate account of what took place. This was the origin of journalism. Another hunter embellished the story to make it more dramatic. This was the origin of theater. The third hunter had a great sense of humor, and he took the same basic story told by the first two hunters and told it in a way that made his fellow tribesmen laugh. This was the origin of stand-up. There was a fourth hunter who did not concern himself with accuracy, drama, or humor. He relayed the story the way the chief of the tribe wanted the story told. That was the origin of Fox News.

Funny stories that comedians perform in clubs are called anecdotal stand-up. These stories can be based on real-life experiences or they can be made up. In either case, there are three keys to transforming a funny story that your friends enjoy into anecdotal stand-up that can entertain a club audience. The three keys are as follows:

1. Building frequent laugh lines into the story by . . .
2. Organizing the story not chronologically but *by subject*, followed by laugh lines that . . .

3. Seem genuine coming from your persona.

We're going to look at each of these keys individually, starting with frequency of laughter. As our example, here is an anecdotal stand-up piece by Hannibal Buress. It's a story about jaywalking in Montreal. The underlines indicate where he gets laughs.

I got a jaywalking ticket in Montreal. I couldn't believe it. I've jaywalked so many times in my life. It's such an easy thing to time out. Is there a car coming? Naw, <u>let me get across there</u>. I've done it thousands of times. But this time it was me and this old lady, <u>we were jaywalking together</u>. <u>We weren't together like that, but if we were, so what, mind your business. I just met y'all.</u> So me and this old lady we get across the street, then a Montreal cop approaches us speaking in French, <u>"BLAHHHH BLAHHH, BLAH, blah blah blah blah blah blah blah blah blah blah blah blah blahlahablahh blahahalahlablablahahla blah. FRENCH."</u> I said, "Hey man, I don't talk like that. That's not how I talk. <u>Can you talk to me how I talk?"</u> <u>That probably wasn't the best way to start off our interaction, by mocking his native language, but who cares, I take risks in life.</u> And he said, "YOU WERE JAYWALKING!" and I said, "Sorry about that." <u>And I try to keep going about my day because I thought that's how jaywalking was handled as a crime</u>: "You were jaywalkin!" "My bad. <u>We're done here, right, that's it.</u> I acknowledge that I jaywalked, I apologize not for the act of jaywalking, <u>but how my jaywalking made you feel.</u> I'll try to not jaywalk in the future while you're watching, but trust I'ma do it the rest of my life, <u>it's the best way to go about being a pedestrian."</u> And he said, "No, I have to give you a ticket, give me your ID!" and I said, "No you don't understand, I only give people my ID for real stuff—this is not real, <u>this is a fantasy crime</u> . . . that you're enforcing, to cover up the fact that your city is having financial problems right now. This city is broke and they put you out here with a quota, and that's fine. <u>I will donate sixty of your colorful-ass</u>

dollars to your broke-ass city, but let's just do it like that, no paperwork. And it's good." Guess what. Two more cops show up. Now we have three Montreal police officers working this high-profile jaywalking case.

The running time of this excerpt is slightly under two minutes. Within that time frame Buress gets 10 solid laughs. When regular storytellers tell a story, there may or may not be laughs along the way. Their story can succeed on the merits of its drama and suspense, with or without laughter. But any form of stand-up that a club comedian employs, including anecdotal stand-up, comes with the challenge and necessity of serving up frequent laughs. Hey, that's why people go to comedy clubs—to laugh.

How do you build so many laughs into one story? Damn good question. Happily, there's an answer. It's our second key to creating funny anecdotal stand-up: organizing the story by subjects, into a series of setup and punchline jokes.

I'll show you how this is done by deconstructing an anecdotal stand-up piece performed by Lenny Bruce.

(Lenny Bruce is considered the father of contemporary stand-up comedy. In his comedy, he fearlessly attacked targets like the Church that were considered absolutely off-limits to mainstream comedians. He spoke about sex with a candor that had never been heard onstage previously. And perhaps most important, he drew on the truth of his life, experiences, opinions, and feelings to a degree that no one had ever seen in stand-up comedy before Lenny Bruce took the mic.)

The first step in deconstructing Bruce's anecdotal stand-up is to lay out the text so you can enjoy it and see how much laughter he has built into the material. This piece is called "Lima, Ohio." You need to know that Lenny Bruce was a very hip, cool, jazzy New York Jewish guy. This excerpt is from a story he performed about what his life was like as a road comic in the early '60s. Another thing you need to know is that it was common in Bruce's day for parks to have Civil War and World War I cannons as monuments. Finally, when Bruce refers to the "Five and Ten," he means the 5- and 10-cent stores, which sold inexpensive items. Once again I've underlined where the audience laughed. In this excerpt, more than 50 percent of the lines in this story are laugh lines. That's a good ratio for stand-up comedy material.

I worked at a place called Lima, Ohio. . . . And I don't know if there are any people in sales here, but when you travel in these towns, there's nothing to do during the day. They're very boring. Like, all right, the <u>first day you go through the Five and Ten, that's one day shot, right?</u> The next day you go to the park, <u>you see the cannon and you've had it. That's it! Forget it.</u> . . . <u>And I'm staying at the Show Business Hotel.</u> The other show people: <u>one guy runs the movie projector in town</u> and the other guy sells <u>Capezio shoes.</u> . . .

. . . And you always hear that small towns are wild . . . it's a dirty lie. Even the waitresses—<u>they're all elderly women with corrective stockings, you know, and Mother Goose shoes and those handkerchiefs, different ones every day, pinned on.</u> I'm looking to swing and <u>they're bringing me jelly and chicken soup. Now, I'm there like the third week and I'm completely whacked.</u> . . . I get off the floor one night, waitress says to me there's a couple who wanna meet you—it's a couple about sixty-five years old, nice people—sit down, they ask me, "You from New York?" I say, "Yeah, originally." . . . They say, "Now listen I'm not kidding you, we got some relations in New York." "Oh really, where?" <u>"Rochester!"</u> <u>"Oh yeah, all right, yeah all right."</u> <u>Now my whole mouth is white from taking the tranquilizer with no water now, you know, and the wife is a real schlub, she's got this short-sleeve dress on with a vaccination as big as a basketball—replete, you know, with a mole with a hair in it</u>—and she's got, you ever seen one of those <u>crinkly dresses, those kind you can see through and you don't wanna!</u>

In order to see the writing structure that makes this 50 percent ratio of laugh lines to straight lines possible, we have to bore down deeper into Bruce's writing.

Most stories are structured chronologically. This happened first, this happened next, and so on. That's not the way comedians organize a story. They do it by subject. This is my first subject, and here are the laugh lines tied to that subject, and here is my second subject and the laugh lines tied to that subject, and so on. Transforming a funny story into stand-up comedy material essentially involves formatting the story in this way.

Let's look at "Lima, Ohio" again. All of the laughs in the first part of the story key off a single subject: small towns like Lima, Ohio, are boring.

Subject 1: "I worked at a place called Lima, Ohio. . . . And I don't know if there are any people in sales here, but when you travel in these towns there's nothing to do during the day. They're very boring."

Punchline 1: "Like, all right, the first day you go through the Five and Ten, that's one day shot, right?"

Punchline 2: "The next day you go to the park, you see the cannon and you've had it."

Punchline 3: "That's it! Forget it. . . ."

Punchline 4: "And I'm staying at the Show Business Hotel. The other show people: one guy runs the movie projector in town and the other guy sells Capezio shoes. . . ."

Debunking the idea that small towns are dens of iniquity is the subject that sets up all of the next laughs.

Subject 2: "And you always hear that small towns are wild . . . it's a dirty lie."

Punchline 1: "Even the waitresses—they're all elderly women with corrective stockings,"

Punchline 2: "you know, and Mother Goose shoes"

Punchline 3: "and those handkerchiefs, different ones every day pinned on."

Punchline 4: "I'm looking to swing and they're bringing me jelly and chicken soup."

Punchline 5: "Now, I'm there like the third week and I'm completely whacked. . . ."

The third subject is that even the people from out of town are boring:

Subject 3: "I get off the floor one night—waitress says to me there's a couple who wanna meet you—it's a couple about sixty-five years old, nice people—sit down, they ask me, "You from New York?" I say, "Yeah, originally." . . . They say, "Now listen I'm not kidding you, we got some relations in New York." "Oh really, where?"

Punchline 1: "Rochester."

Punchline 2: "Oh yeah, all right, yeah all right."

Punchline 3: "Now my whole mouth is white from taking the tranquilizer with no water now, you know,"

Punchline 4: "and the wife is a real schlub,"

Punchline 5: "she's got this short-sleeve dress on with a vaccination as big as a basketball"

Punchline 6: "—replete, you know, with a mole with a hair in it—"

Punchline 7: "and she's got, you ever seen one of those crinkly dresses, those kind you can see through and you don't wanna!"

Lenny's audience laughed throughout the story because he organized it by subjects (setups) with multiple punchlines.

The first two stories in this chapter leave us feeling that they actually happened. There may be some exaggeration, some comedic license taken with the facts. But clearly Hannibal Buress and Lenny Bruce intended for us to believe that their stories actually occurred.

It's also possible to successfully create anecdotal stand-up about events that are made up. What makes these pieces work is our third key to creating funny anecdotal stand-up: the story feels genuine because it fits the comedian's persona.

An example of this comes from a fanciful and hilarious piece of anecdotal stand-up by Dino Wiand, a new comedian and a student of mine. The following excerpt is the beginning of his story about flying from one New York City airport to another New York City airport. What you need to know is that Dino lives near JFK Airport and has gotten a job near LaGuardia Airport, which is about a half-hour car ride away. The crazy, fanciful part of this story is that Dino is convinced it would be more convenient to fly to LaGuardia from JFK even though both airports are in the same city, a short car ride away from each other. In the excerpt, you can see that Dino has successfully applied the first key: the material gets frequent laughs. Dino also employed the second key: he organized the material by subjects (setups) and punchlines (laugh lines). His first subject is deciding to fly from JFK to LaGuardia; his second subject is that the in-flight movie is boring.

You can fly anywhere in the world from New York JFK Airport. But you cannot fly to New York's LaGuardia Airport. Which is a shame, because I live by JFK and I just got a job at LaGuardia. I discovered that you can only fly from JFK to LaGuardia if you change planes. And according to Expedia.com it costs $735, one way, on United Airlines. It's a four-hour flight from JFK to Denver, Colorado . . . then a five-hour layover in Denver, then it's a four-hour-and-fifteen-minute flight from Denver to LaGuardia. I took the red-eye because I wanted to be at work nice and early.

So when I got on the flight from JFK to Denver, I couldn't believe how horrible the entertainment was. On the in-flight system they were showing a movie called, I think, *Map Details.* It's about a plane that flies actually from JFK to Denver. It's terrible animation. I don't know what Hollywood was doing with this thing. It's like a waste of money. But anyway, I was watching it, bored out of my mind, for four hours. And then they turned it off just as we came into Denver and I missed the ending.

In good anecdotal stand-up the characters in the story are recognizable and their behavior is believable, even if the premise of the story is fanciful. Audiences laugh when the story matches up with the personality of the comedian telling the story. Dino's persona is clear: he is mind-bogglingly clueless. Before he tells this story, he opens with jokes that vividly establish his persona. For example:

> I tried to divorce my wife last year, but she told me that we got divorced fifteen years ago. I said, "When were you going to tell me?!!!" She said, "I did, fifteen years ago when we got divorced." And then she went on and on about, I don't know, something about me not listening to her.

As loopy as the airport story is, it engages the audience, and they laugh because they recognize that, as unlikely as this story is, it could happen to Dino.

A story with frequent laughs, organized as a series of setup and punchline jokes, that feels genuine because it fits the comedian's persona—that, my friend, is anecdotal stand-up.

6

THE STAND-UP SKETCH

THE STAND-UP SKETCH BECAME PROMINENT in the 1950s and 1960s when the theater was, more so than now, at the center of our arts and entertainment scene. Theater influenced comedians like Shelly Berman and Bob Newhart, who became enormously popular by writing and performing stand-up sketches. A stand-up sketch is essentially a one-person play where you act out all the parts. The comedian enacts the characters until the scene ends. He does not interrupt the scene with comments made as himself. It's an uninterrupted performance of a single scene.

The theatrical comedian Eddie Izzard is a master of the stand-up sketch. Here is an excerpt from his "Star Wars Cantina" piece. He sets it up simply by positing that the Death Star must have had someplace to eat, a cafeteria. In the performance, he creates two characters. The first is Darth Vader, for whom Izzard uses a deep, commanding voice. The second is a cafeteria worker who refuses to serve Vader food unless he takes a tray. Izzard plays the cafeteria worker as an ordinary guy who knows the rules and has no intention of waiving them just because his customer's name is Darth Vader. Izzard creates comedy in the sketch by showing the imperious Vader's growing frustration and confusion in dealing with this officious menial. The underlines indicate where he gets laughs.

VADER: I will have the penne all'arrabbiata.

CAFETERIA WORKER: You'll need a tray.

VADER: Do you know who I am?

CAFETERIA WORKER: Do you know who I am?

VADER: This is not a game of who-the-fuck-are-you. For I am Vader. Darth Vader. Lord Vader. I can kill you with a single thought.

CAFETERIA WORKER: Well, you'll still need a tray.

VADER: No, I will not need a tray, I do not need a tray to kill you. I can kill you without a tray, with the power of the Force, which is strong within me, even though I could kill you with a tray if I so wished. For I would hack at your neck with a thin bit until the blood flowed across the canteen floor.

CAFETERIA WORKER: No, the food is hot; you'll need a tray to put the food on.

VADER: Oh I see, the food is hot—I'm sorry I did not realize. Ha ha ahh ha ha oh, yes . . . I thought you were challenging me to a fight to the death.

CAFETERIA WORKER: Fight to the death? This is the canteen, I work here.

VADER: Yes but I am Vader. I am Lord Vader. Everyone challenges me to a fight to the death. Lord, Darth Vader, I'm Darth Vader, Lord Sir Lord Vader, Sir Lord Darth Vader, Lord Darth, Sir Lord Vader of Cheam, Sir Lord Baron Von Vaderham, the Death Star, I run the Death Star.

CAFETERIA WORKER: What's the Death Star?

VADER: This is the Death Star. You're in the Death Star. I run this star.

CAFETERIA WORKER: This is a star?

VADER: This is a fucking star, I run it. I'm your boss.

CAFETERIA WORKER: You're Mr. Stevens?

VADER: No, who is Mr. Stevens?

CAFETERIA WORKER: He's head of catering.

VADER: I'm not head of catering, I am Vader, I can kill catering with a thought.

CAFETERIA WORKER: What?

VADER: I can kill you all. I can kill me with a thought, just, fuck—I'll get a tray.

This chapter wouldn't be complete without an excerpt from Bob Newhart, the grand master of the stand-up sketch. Newhart achieved an extraordinary level of success in stand-up and on television. In 1960, his album *The Button-Down Mind of Bob Newhart* became the first comedy album to place number one on the *Billboard* charts, outselling Elvis Presley. On television, he starred in two massively popular sitcoms, one right after the other: *The Bob Newhart Show* in the 1970s and *Newhart* in the 1980s. The stand-up sketches he performed on his legendary album launched him into stardom.

We're going to look at an excerpt from his piece "The Driving Instructor." You need to know that Newhart had a deadpan delivery. He expressed alarm with just a slight stammer. Whereas Eddie Izzard played both characters in a two-character sketch, in this two-character sketch Newhart plays only one. His writing and performing make it clear what the other character in the sketch is saying and doing. Newhart sets this piece up by saying it's the first episode of a documentary series he's doing on people who risk their lives every day at their jobs—driving instructors. He asks the audience to imagine that he's a driving instructor seated in a car next to his student. The underlines indicate—you get the underlines by now, right?

How do you do? Ahh, you're Mrs. Webb, is that right? Oh I see, you've had one lesson already. Who was the instructor on that, Mrs. Webb? Mr. Adam, I-I'm sorry, here it is: Mr. Adams. Just let me read ahead and kind of familiarize myself with the case. Um, how fast were you going when Mr. Adams jumped from the car? Seventy-five? And where was that? In your driveway? How far had Mr. Adams gotten in the lesson? Backing out? I see, you were backing out at seventy-five and that's when he, that's when he jumped. Did he cover starting the car? And the other way of stopping? Uh, what's the other way of stopping? Throwing it in reverse. Oh that would do it, you're right, that would do it. All right, you want to start the car? Uh, Mrs. Webb, you just turned on the lights. You want to start the car? They all look alike, don't they? I don't know why they design them that way, um. All right, let's pull out into traffic. Now what's the first thing we're going to do before we pull out into traffic? What did Mr. Adams do before he let you pull out into traffic? Well I mean, <u>besides praying, let's say</u>. No, what I had in mind was checking the rearview mirror . . . you see we always want to check the rear—<u>DON'T PULL OUT!!!!!!</u>

The characteristics of a successful stand-up sketch are similar to those of anecdotal stand-up: we laugh a lot, the sketch is a series of setup and punchline jokes, and the sketch fits the comedian's persona. Eddie Izzard, who appears in high heels and makeup, is a highly theatrical and commanding onstage presence. We believe him as Darth Vader and we believe him as the cafeteria worker who will give no ground. Newhart's emotionally understated, shy, polite persona is perfect for the nice driving instructor who continues with his lesson even though his pupil's incompetence as a driver could kill him.

The successful stand-up sketch has an additional key: its premise is believable. It's believable that the Death Star would have a cafeteria to feed the hundreds of people on board. It's believable that a driving instructor might have a terrible student.

There's something else really important that I want you to know about this form. As a delivery system for laugh lines, the stand-up sketch can't be beat. Once the initial setup is in place, the rest of the piece can be virtually all punchlines, nonstop laughs. The Izzard excerpt, for example, takes 2 minutes and 10 seconds to perform. Within that time frame, he gets 18 laughs. All of them key off one setup: the Death Star had to have someplace to eat.

7

ACT-OUTS

AT THIS POINT YOU MAY BE THINKING, *Wow, I really like observational and I love anecdotal and I have a great idea for a stand-up sketch. Which one should I choose? This is a dilemma!* Actually it's not. It's always a happy moment for me when I can bring you good news. So it's with a heart full of joy that I tell you that there is no dilemma. Comedians partake of all the forms described in this book. The forms are not mutually exclusive. For example, one piece of material may be part observational and part anecdotal, and also include what are called *act-outs*. Think of the forms as threads that you use to weave your comic tapestry. In this chapter on act-outs, I'll show you how this is done.

Act-outs are another form of stand-up where the comedian acts out other characters or himself in a scene. Here's the difference between act-outs and a stand-up sketch.

(If you are a teacher and are using this book as a text for your students, first of all, thank you. Second of all, you must swear on all you hold sacred that you will never give your students a written test which asks what the difference is between an act-out and a stand-up sketch. My purpose in classifying the forms of stand-up comedy is practical and not academic. Knowledge of the forms gives comedians and comedy writers options, choices on how to give shape to their comic ideas. If you want to know if your students understand the forms, don't ask them to tell you about them. Ask them to show you. For example, have them create and perform an act-out and a stand-up sketch. You'll know that your students have learned the forms when you see your students perform them. If you're not a teacher, you didn't need to read this bit. Sorry.)

A stand-up sketch begins with the comedian explaining to the audience what the premise of the sketch is—for instance, there has to be a place to eat on the Death Star. Once he's accomplished this he launches into the sketch and performs it from the beginning to its conclusion. At no point does he stop enacting the sketch to chat with the audience. In an act-out, however, he *does* break out of the scene to talk to the audience. And when he's done with the chat, he either returns to the scene, acts out a different scene, or changes the subject altogether.

We'll see how this is done by looking at an excerpt of a Louis C.K. piece called "Monopoly." It's a hilarious example of act-outs. It's also an example of employing several of the stand-up forms in one piece of material.

Louis starts his "Monopoly" piece with observational jokes, then does an act-out of himself sweetly consoling his daughter about her loss in the board game Candy Land. He then comes out of the act-out and, in a chat with the audience, sets up a second act-out of a different scene. In this act-out, he taunts his daughter about losing at Monopoly.

Here is how to read this piece: You know about the underlines. Words in italics indicate observational jokes; boldfaced words indicate act-outs.

I play Monopoly with my kids; that's really fun. My nine-year-old, she can totally do Monopoly. The six-year-old actually totally gets how the game works, *but she's not emotionally developed enough to handle her <u>inevitable loss</u> <u>in every game of Monopoly</u>. Because the Monopoly loss <u>is dark</u>, <u>it's heavy</u>.* It's not like when you lose at, you know, Candy Land, **"Ohh, you got stuck <u>in the fudgy thing</u>, baby! Oh well, you're <u>in the gummy</u>**

twirly o's and you didn't get to win." But when she loses
in Monopoly I gotta look at her little face and I go . . . "OK,
so here's what's going to happen now, OK? All your property . . . everything you have . . . all your railroads, your
houses, all your money . . . that's mine now. Gotta give it
all to me. Give it to me. That's right. And no, no you can't
play anymore, see, because even though you're giving me
all of that? It doesn't even touch how much you owe me.
Doesn't even touch it, baby. You're going down hard, it's
really bad. All you've been working for all day, I'm gonna
take it now . . . and I'm going to use it to destroy your sister.
I mean I'm gonna ruin her. It's just mayhem on this board
for her now."

It's hard to imagine this piece having nearly the same comic
impact if Louis chose merely to describe this scene with his daughter
rather than acting it out. The change in tone of his voice from the
loving dad playing Candy Land to the cold-blooded capitalist playing Monopoly creates much of the comedy. This would be lost in
a description. Which brings me to a good general guideline about
writing comedy: it is better to show the audience something than it
is to tell them about it. Let them see it. It's almost always funnier. A
great rewriting technique for a joke that is almost there, but needs
punching up, is to retell it through act-outs.

Marina Franklin is a stand-up who extensively performs act-outs
to bring to life a wide range of characters. Franklin originally came
to New York to become an actor but went on to become one of the
best stand-ups of her generation. The skill she acquired as an actor to
transform herself into other characters is put to hilarious use in her
stand-up performances. As an example, here is an excerpt from her
piece about arriving in New York and performing in a play in front
of an all-black audience. To get the comedy in this piece you need to
know that Marina is African American and, as she tells her audience,
growing up she was the only black kid in an all-white neighborhood
in Chicago. Then her family moved to an all-black neighborhood.

But as Marina puts it, "It was too late. I was white." In this piece she acts out five characters: herself, herself playing a part in the play, another actress in the play, a woman in the audience, and a woman behind the counter at a restaurant. She performs each character with a distinctive voice. She and the other actress sound like well-trained actors performing the roles of two college-educated African American sisters. The woman in the audience and the woman behind the counter have Brooklyn street dialects. Once again, the italics indicate observational jokes, boldfaced words indicate act-outs, and underlined words indicate—oh my God, you know this.

I came to New York originally to do theater but it didn't work out. *I did a play off off Broadway, like Brooklyn. Bed Stuy . . . you could call it Bed Stuy, Broadway.* I played this character <u>Shashu Aiesha</u>. This revolutionary sister. It was a hard play to do too because it was an all-black audience and you know, we like to get involved. You know, and I had this line in the play where I tell my sister, because her husband just gets out of jail, so I say to her in the play I say: **"Maybe if you hadn't have put so many unreasonable material demands on this man . . . this might not have ever happened."** I was in my moment onstage, this girl got up from the audience she's like, <u>**"UH-UH. You need to slap that bitch."**</u> I was like, <u>**"It's a play!"**</u> **"Can someone tell <u>her</u> I'm acting?"** I remember later on in the play the girl who plays my sister she accuses me of being in love with her husband. So her line is, she says to me, **"I can tell from the way you spoke his name. I can tell from the music in your voice when you spoke his name."** And that same girl got up from the audience, she's like, <u>**"UUUHH HUH, I heard it too."**</u> *That's Brooklyn for you.* I remember being out there I was constantly trying to find like salads, and everything was fried. And I went to this one place to try to get a salad and I get this girl behind the counter with the attitude. I'm like, "Can I get a salad?" She's like <u>**"Uh-uh, we ain't got that."**</u> I'm like, "I see salad on the menu." <u>**"Well, I said we ain't got that."**</u> Then I see

her going to the back **"Tisha. Tisha, come here for a second.
Ain't that that same bitch we saw in that play?"**

In Louis C.K.'s "Monopoly" piece, act-outs provide comic fire-power to intimate scenes with his daughter. In Franklin's piece, they empower her to quickly and gracefully shift characters and scenes. In the club, there is only Marina on a bare stage. But through her act-outs she transports us first to a theater in Brooklyn with two actors onstage, an all-black audience, and someone in the audience calling out; and then to a restaurant in the same neighborhood with Marina and a woman behind the counter. The piece has the scope and flow of a movie. Act-outs make this happen.

If you enjoy playing other characters and doing character voices, employ stand-up sketches and act-outs in your material.

8

PUT-DOWN HUMOR— CELEBRITY PUT-DOWNS

PUT-DOWN HUMOR IS COMEDY that gets laughs by putting someone down, making fun of them. Put-down humor has five targets:

- Celebrities
- People in your life (your significant other, parents, siblings, the guy who dry-cleans your shirts, etc.)
- Hecklers in your audience
- Innocent people in your audience
- And, of course, yourself

I've encountered people who have difficulty with the idea of making fun of others. They believe it's not nice. And, of course, they're right. But here's the thing: comedy is not nice. It is unflinchingly, unapologetically *honest*. Comedy looks unblinkingly at life and says, "A lot of this sucks. Let me be specific." And a lot of life does suck. Always has, always will. Comedy is an entertainment that calls out the bad stuff. It ridicules the bad stuff. By taking the things we struggle with and worry about, and by ridiculing these things, comedy transforms them from overwhelming to laughable. It enables us to laugh at the struggles and problems we share. And when we can laugh, we know we're OK. And when we hear other people in the room laugh, we know we're not alone. For a glorious moment the comedian lifts our worries off our shoulders and unites us in laughter. The underlying message of comedy is this: You have problems; I have problems. But we're OK. You are not alone. We're in this damn thing together.

Comedy has a much higher purpose than being nice. It helps us survive. So swing away.

Putting down celebrities is a perennial staple of stand-up comedy. It's eternally satisfying to watch the super rich, the super powerful, the super famous cut down to their human size by a smart, insightful comedian.

There are two keys to creating successful celebrity-put-down jokes. The first is to be sure your famous people are famous, that your audience knows who they are. You may have hilarious jokes about the Secretary of Commerce, but no one knows who this person is or even if we have one. New comedians who are sports fans are often startled when they discover that club audiences don't recognize sports figures who are well known to die-hard fans but not to people who don't follow sports. Comedians who are political junkies are surprised when their Orrin Hatch jokes flop. (He's the senior senator from Utah, and a Republican. Unless you're performing in Utah, no one really knows or cares.) You need to pick targets who are front and center in the media day after day. The audience won't laugh if they don't know who you're talking about.

The second key is that your reason for ridiculing the celebrity must also be known to your audience, and they have to agree with you about it. It is sometimes said that comedians write the first draft of history. This isn't so. The audience only laughs when they already know the history, and when they know that what you're saying is true.

Most of the time people laugh because they're surprised by what you say. This isn't the case with celebrity put-down jokes. They laugh out of the pleasure, the joy they take in hearing the truth. For eight and a half years, audiences laughed at George W. Bush jokes that had the exact same premise: he was stupid and struggled with the

English language, the only language he spoke. There were no surprises in these jokes, yet thousands of them were successful. Likewise, Bill Clinton's philandering was the premise of jokes for his two terms as president, and beyond.

To repeat: the person and the reason for ridiculing him or her must be well known, and the audience must agree with you. People would be mystified at jokes about Bill Clinton being dumb or George Bush being a philanderer. For a celebrity put-down joke to work, a famous person must be lined up with his or her most famously recognizable foible. When that happens, you can go to town. For example:

> Overall, Bush's European trip has been an overwhelming success. Not once has he gotten separated from his group.
>
> —David Letterman

> As you know, President Bush is on a tour of Europe; he says he's hoping to see the whole country.
>
> —Jay Leno

> President Clinton apparently gets so much action that every couple of weeks they have to spray WD-40 on his zipper.
>
> —David Letterman

> On Tuesday NBC's news special "Inside the Obama White House" was watched by nine million people. Historians say it was the most revealing look behind the scenes at the White House since Bill Clinton set up a secret webcam.
>
> —Conan O'Brien

We all know who the president is, and if the media reports on his foibles, we all know about those as well. That's why presidents are staples of put-down jokes. There were very few Obama jokes because there wasn't a national consensus about his foibles. The attacks on him have been partisan ones concerning his policies, not consensus opinions about his personal shortcomings. An intelligent, hard-working, well-informed president who is a devoted husband and father simply isn't that funny, even if you disagree with his policies. Donald Trump is a different story. His lack of government experience, his multiple marriages, his mop of orange hair, and his egomania were fodder for countless jokes even before he became president:

> You know, all of Donald Trump's wives have come from other countries as immigrants. That just shows you that women are still coming to this country to do the jobs that Americans don't wanna do.
>
> —George Lopez

> Donald Trump showed his birth certificate to reporters. Who cares about his birth certificate? I want to know if that thing on his head has had its vaccinations.
>
> —Craig Ferguson

> Yes, Trump is unstoppable. He's like Godzilla with less foreign policy experience.
>
> —Stephen Colbert

Pop celebrities are also staples of put-down humor. But again, they can't just be famous; they have to have a famous foible. That was the case when Michael Jackson went to trial for the alleged sexual abuse of a 13-year-old boy. There had already been widespread rumors that Jackson was a pedophile. The trial created a national consensus that there was truth to the rumors. This caused a torrent of Jackson jokes, none more intelligent or funnier than Chris Rock's. In this excerpt the laughs are underlined, words in italics indicate observational jokes, and boldfaced words indicate act-outs.

Michael Jackson lost his mind. What the hell is wrong with Michael? *Another kid! Another kid!!!!* I thought it was Groundhog's Day when I heard that shit. Another kid?! Get the fuck outta here. Yo, that's how much we love Michael. *We love Michael so much, we let the first kid slide.* Another kid! I'm fuckin' done. I'm done with Michael! I'm done, I was a fan my whole life, I am fuckin' done. I'm handing in my glove. OK. I saw Michael on *60 Minutes . . . Ed Bradley tried his best to make Michael look like a mammal.* Somebody that drank water and breathed air, right? *He gave Michael the easiest questions in the world. The easiest GED questions in the world and Michael could not pass the test.* He's like: **"Uhh, Michael. Do you think it's proper for a forty-five-year-old man to sleep in a bed with thirteen-year-old boys?"** (Chris answers as Michael with a huge smile) "Yes!" "OK, OK, uh, let me rephrase that. Uhh, Michael, would you let your children sleep in the bed of a forty-five-year-old man that's been accused of child molestation? (Chris as Michael with huge smile) "Yes!"** *Ed Bradley looked at Michael Jackson like he wanted to say, "Nigga, is you crazy!?"*

There's one caveat about celebrity put-down jokes: they have a limited shelf life. After a while, people have heard enough, and it's time to move on to the next train wreck. During the Clinton administration there were endless jokes about Monica Lewinsky, who performed fellatio on the president and had the stain on her dress to prove it. Way more interesting than Orrin Hatch, right? But I remember a sad night at Carolines shortly after Clinton left office when a good Monica Lewinsky joke fell flat. I remember thinking that night, *Damn, this party is finally over.*

I'm writing this book in a time when there are a lot of bad feelings about our country: our government is dysfunctional, our political system has been corrupted by big money, our health care system is a mess, and we're falling behind the rest of the world in the paramount job of educating our young. I can, however, report to you some good news about our country. I've learned from working with comedians from all over the world—Europe, Asia, Africa, the Middle East, Australia, New Zealand, North and South and Latin America—that there is no place on Earth that surpasses the US when it comes to freedom of speech. I work with comedians who live in democracies that will not tolerate criticism of the government. I work with comedians who live in democracies where their lives have been threatened, not because of anything that they're saying onstage, but because they are Muslim women performing stand-up.

There's a lot that's wrong with this place, and there are some things that are amazingly right about it. Freedom of speech is one of those right things. If you are of a mind to, exercise it, baby.

9

PUT-DOWN HUMOR—
PEOPLE IN YOUR LIFE

You in a personal struggle is the golden land of comedy. For that reason, creating stand-up about the struggles you're having with people in your life is a mighty fine idea. I want you to be aware from the outset, however, that doing this kind of put-down humor comes with a major caveat: Don't make the assumption that the audience is on your side when you complain about people they don't know. For them to laugh at your jokes, you have to get them on your side first. Starting a joke with, "My girlfriend is an asshole," is a very bad idea. We don't know her. We hardly know you. If she's an asshole, why is she your girlfriend? What kind of person calls his girlfriend an asshole? An asshole, that's who. *Yeah, you're the asshole, you asshole.* That's not what you want your audience thinking.

Let me give you a real-life example. Every once in a blue moon I produce a stand-up show where the audience starts laughing and they never stop. Every single joke from every stand-up gets a huge laugh. The audience is in stitches. They're hysterical with laughter. The waitstaff are getting laughs taking orders. We were having a night like this at the club Don't Tell Mama. Every stand-up is killing it, and then this guy gets onstage and, with his first setup, he shuts down the turbines of laughter. A quiet descends on 46th Street between Broadway and Eighth that I didn't think possible to experience anywhere in Midtown Manhattan. I thought that only Tibetan monks isolated on distant outcrops of the Himalayas could experience such absolute, total silence. Here's what he said:

> Good evening. I work in a club just like this one, and the people who go to these clubs are assholes.

So he opens up by calling each of us in his audience an asshole. Here is a trade secret: people don't like that. Here is what he was supposed to say:

> Good evening. I work in a club just like this one, and you wouldn't believe what some people do when they're watching a show.

All of us have sat near someone at a show who does something annoying like loudly unwrapping a piece of candy, or talking back to the movie screen, or doing what the guy who sat next to me at the New York Philharmonic was doing as the orchestra began the exquisite overture to the musical *Carousel*. He started loudly humming along. It's fun to laugh at jokes about such people. But if you call *me* an asshole, I'm not laughing.

Rodney Dangerfield was a master of put-down humor. Like Chris Rock in his Michael Jackson piece, Dangerfield positions his put-downs of other people as struggles for himself. His wife was a constant target:

> The other day I got back from a business trip. I got in a cab and told the driver, "Hey! Take me where the action is." He took me home!

> Last week my wife told me that she was going to cut me down to twice a month. But I thought about it, and I figured that

it wasn't too bad. I know a couple of guys that she cut out completely.

Where you see Dangerfield's skill as a comedy writer is in the way he tees these jokes up. He doesn't start by saying, "My wife is a slut." He starts with, "I get no respect." With that short, famous refrain of his, he gets us on his side and enables us to laugh at his wife's supposed philandering.

Phyllis Diller is another great stand-up who famously put down her spouse. She always referred to him by the nickname she gave him, Fang:

> If your husband gets fired as often as Fang, I will pass on this important tip. When he calls and says he's bringing the boss home to dinner, don't start getting it ready until 5:30.

> I was sort of tricked into marrying. One night I was out with Fang and a girl said, "You better hold on to him." I thought I had a prize. I didn't know she meant that after one drink he falls down.

The same comedic strategy is at work: Diller makes Fang's shortcomings a struggle for herself.

Louis C.K. appears to be an exception to the rule that to get laughs by putting people down, you first need to get the audience on your side. He tees up his jokes about his children by heaping abuse on them:

> The other kid we have is a—she's a girl and she's four and she's also a fucking asshole. Uhh, it's true, man, I'm serious. I say that with no remorse. Fucking asshole. She's a douchebag. She is! Fuckin' jerk. The other day I'm like, "Put your shoes on we're trying to leave. Put your shoes on please, put your shoes on. Put your shoes on." How many times can you say that to somebody before you just want to kick them right in

the fuckin' face. Seriously. If you're with a group of people who are trying to go somewhere and you can't go, you can't go, because a member of your party just refuses to put their shoes on . . . that person is a fuckin' asshole. OK? You don't do that to people. Imagine being with a group: "**Hey, we can't go.**" "Why?" "Because fuckin' **Bill won't put his shoes on, he just won't put them on.**" "Fuck. Bill, what's your problem?" "**I don't want to put 'em on.**" "**Fuck you!**"

Louis C.K. is famous for speaking the unspeakable, and nowhere is that clearer than in his jokes about his daughters. He gets laughs on the shock value of verbally abusing them. But look closely at these jokes and you'll see the same strategy in place. His daughter's typical four-year-old behavior—in this case refusing to put her shoes on—causes a struggle for him. What gives these jokes freshness is his attitude to this common, recognizable parental frustration. It makes him furious. What makes him edgy is that he expresses his rage.

This excerpt provides an insight into how skilled stand-ups build originality into their material. It's not original for stand-ups to talk about their young children's intransigence. But although the subject is not original, Louis's emotional take on this subject is. He's not benignly frustrated and amused by it. He's furious about it. He takes her behavior very, very personally, and in so doing embraces the principle that a personal struggle is comedy's golden land. In this original way, he succeeds in getting his audience on his side so we can laugh at his put-downs.

Many new stand-ups don't understand Louis C.K.'s work. They hear him curse, so they curse. They hear him say outrageous things, so they do too. What they don't see is the comedy-writing craftsmanship that underlies his jokes and makes them hilarious to large audiences. If you want to write jokes like Louis C.K., master the crafts of writing and performing stand-up comedy and apply those crafts to creating jokes that take a fresh approach to taboo subjects that genuinely matter to you.

10

PUT-DOWN HUMOR—
HECKLERS

COMEDY CLUB AUDIENCES ARE ENCOURAGED to drink alcohol during the show. This creates profits for the club and also helps create a feeling of fun and conviviality in the audience. And on occasion, it creates hecklers. This chapter will teach you how to handle these loathsome sots.

The first step is to make sure you've got a heckler and not some person who may be calling out things inappropriately but who is enjoying your performance. A person calling out "Oh my God, that is so funny!" is not a heckler. A person calling out "Sit down, Jew boy, you're not funny!" is. A heckler is someone who is insulting you in a voice that others can hear. It's important that you make this distinction between hecklers and loudmouth non-hecklers because you're going to nuke a heckler with biting, comedic insults. You don't want to nuke someone whose inhibitions may be down because he or she had too much to drink but who is enjoying your set. I wrote heckler jokes for a comedian who, when he read them in my office, loved them. He loved them so much that he used them onstage at his next performance. He came out and asked the audience, "How you guys doing?" Someone in the audience said, "Great! Terrific! Never felt better!" With that, the comedian unleashed the heckler jokes to the utter bafflement of the audience. *Why is this guy insulting someone who is just answering his question? What a jerk.* Thus my comedian committed hara-kiri in the opening 30 seconds of his act. After the show I thanked him for admiring the heckler jokes I'd written, but urged him to, next time, wait until he's heckled to use them.

So, step one is to make sure the loudmouth is a heckler. Here is step two: the first time the heckler insults you, don't respond. Let it go. You're going to do this because you want to give the heckler rope to hang himself. People don't like hecklers. They've come to hear you, not some inebriated moron. By not responding the first time, you get the audience squarely on your side. Now they're ready for you to give this margarita-soaked bully his or her comeuppance. Having let the first one go, if the heckler interrupts you again, feel free to annihilate him. The important thing at this moment is to have good material.

Which brings us to step three: have material prepared for this situation. When you are heckled onstage, it makes you angry. You've been insulted. Your heart may start pounding. You want what comes out of your mouth to destroy the heckler, not you. In this viral age, when comedians mishandle a heckler the consequences can damage their careers.

It gives me no pleasure to give you the clearest example of this I know. It involves Michael Richards, the profoundly funny actor who played Kramer on *Seinfeld.* Some time after the series ended, Richards was performing stand-up at the Laugh Factory in L.A. He was heckled by an African American audience member who called out to him that he wasn't funny. This triggered a vicious racist rant from Richards. It went viral and became a national scandal. Richards publicly apologized, but although it was clear he deeply regretted what had come out of his mouth that night, the damage to his career was done—damage that has been long lasting.

Let's review. First, make sure the person is a heckler. Second, get the audience on your side by not responding at first. Third, have heckler jokes ready that *keep* them on your side.

Your heckler material should do two things: First, it should get the audience laughing at the heckler's expense; hecklers need to discover there is a price to be paid for their rudeness. Second, it should send a message to the heckler to shut up. If you don't include that message, the heckler may feel that you're inviting him to go tit for tat with you.

T. J. Miller's act was interrupted by someone in the balcony yelling something unintelligible at him. Miller asked her to repeat what she said. She didn't; she was silent. Here was Miller's reply:

> It's so weird when people yell something and then when you're like, "What did you just say?" they say, "AAH, I don't talk when it's customarily appropriate to talk. . . . For instance in response to a question. No I only speak when a group of strangers has come together to tacitly agree that they won't speak while another one speaks into a device that is specifically to amplify his voice—THAT'S when I speak."

Ricky Gervais had this to say to a heckler:

> This is a big venue. I can't really get into one-to-ones. In a smaller room I'd still ignore you—shut up!

These jokes are mean, funny, and fitting given the hecklers' rudeness, and they carry out both steps of good heckler material.

To help you come up with heckler jokes, here is a list of what hecklers say the most:

1. *You're not funny.*
2. *That's not funny.*
3. *You're ugly.*
4. *Get off the stage, you [insert racial, ethnic, religious, sexual slur here—e.g., Jew boy, guinea, Polack].*
5. *(To a woman) Show me your boobs.*
6. *Where did you get those boobs?*
7. Anything else that includes the word *boobs.*

Jokes that can be used against hecklers in almost any situation key off these notions:

1. Stop interrupting me. *I conduct my act the same way you conduct your sex life—alone.*
2. You're ugly. *Is that your face or are you going to a Halloween party later?*
3. You're stupid. *You shouldn't be here. Didn't they tell you that to be in this club you need to be an adult and have a brain?*
4. You're a loser. *I'm working and you're interrupting me. I wouldn't do that to you. I wouldn't go to your place of employment and hold your mop.*
5. Shut up. *Shut up.*

For some well-prepared comedians, a heckler can be manna from heaven. You get the biggest laughs when audiences think you've come up with something funny on the spot. When you deliver a prepared heckler joke your audience thinks you're being spontaneously funny. They think because you couldn't have known you'd be heckled, you couldn't have prepared your hilarious response.

In a well-run comedy club, there are security people. I call them "Gorillas in the Mist." Somebody gets out of line at the club, and suddenly a very large man is there. In a well-produced show, the producer will see how you're doing with the heckler. If he sees you are scoring and enjoying yourself, he'll let you handle the situation. If he sees things are getting out of hand, he'll have the "gorillas" escort the heckler out of the club.

It's important that you know that, ultimately, you have the power when you're being heckled. The audience is there to hear you, not the heckler. Because you and only you have the microphone, you can totally dominate the conversation. You can write material that completely outguns your opponent. And if you've had it with a heckler, you can ask security to take him or her out. The heckler can't ask security to take you out.

You have the power. Use it wisely.

11

PUT-DOWN HUMOR—
INSULT COMEDY

INSULT COMEDY IS A FORM OF STAND-UP COMEDY aimed at non-hecklers in your audience. These are polite, innocent people who perhaps are late to the show and are getting seated during your set; or perhaps they get up during your set because they need to use the restroom or take a call; or perhaps their phone goes off during your performance; or perhaps they haven't done a thing. Perhaps they've been smiling at you and laughing at your jokes all night. Such people can be wellsprings of comedy.

The way of dealing with these people is different from the way you deal with hecklers. These people are not insulting you. So if you started venomously insulting them, you would lose the audience. It would be uncalled for. When you aim jokes at innocent people, the audience must clearly get from you that behind your insult jokes are feelings of fun and camaraderie.

There are comedians whose entire acts are insult comedy. The grand master of this form was Don Rickles, known ironically as "Mr. Warmth" because he had nothing good to say about anyone. But when you were in his audience you could feel Rickles radiating affection toward the very people he was insulting. He was the warmest comedian I've ever seen. It was his combination of insults and affection that made him an abiding star, beloved by generations of fans, including me. His appearances on *The Tonight Show with Johnny Carson* were, for me, the ultimate must-see TV. When I went to see him perform live in the Bay Area in the early '70s, a fervently wished-for dream of mine came true: Rickles called me a hockey puck.

Identifying the categories of Rickles's insult jokes can help you create your own insult jokes. One category is race/ethnicity/nationality. Here is Rickles (who served in the US Navy during World War II) addressing a Japanese member of his audience:

> Chinese? Filipino? Japanese! Three years in the jungle, looking for your uncle!

Rickles, finding out someone is Mexican:

> I swear to God my wife and I were in Mexico City for two weeks, we never saw the city. She kept saying (running across the stage as if he was trying to hold in diarrhea), "I think it's the salad!"

Rickles at the Just for Laughs comedy festival in Montreal, putting down Canada by reprimanding his band leader for a musical mistake:

> Stop the goddamn band. For Chrissake, it's wrong. This is Montreal. You've got to do good. If you do good here you go right to Saskatchewan.

On learning that an audience member's name is Mitzel:

> (Speaking in a German accent, Rickles raises his arm in a Nazi salute.) Good to see you. (Seated in a chair, he lifts his legs as if he was doing the Nazi goose step.) Remember the old days, Mitzel? (To the audience) No wonder he didn't want to tell me his name.

Another category of Rickles's insult jokes is a person's age and appearance. To a man seated with his wife:

> Is that your wife, sir? (Finding out she is, Rickles closes his eyes as if he cannot bear to see what he's looking at.) Jesus Chri— No, I'm kidding, she's a pretty lady. (Closing his eyes again) Jesus. What was it, a train? (With the mic he makes sound of train hitting something.)

The third category for Rickles was famous people either in his audience or with whom he was sharing the stage. He was at his funniest when he insulted the renowned and powerful. Here is an excerpt of Rickles when he made an unannounced appearance on *The Tonight Show with Johnny Carson* and went after Johnny's superstar guest Frank Sinatra. Sinatra's power in the entertainment business was summed up by his nickname, "the Chairman of the Board." It was rumored that Sinatra had mob connections. No one in show business dared to confront the Chairman with this rumor. No one but Rickles:

> Marco Mangananzo was hurt. Fambino Bombazzo (punches fist into other hand), two bullets in the head, Thursday. Now this, this you don't believe. Excuse us Johnny, you're from the Midwest, you're busy going **"IS THE TRUCK LOADED?!"** Guido says hi. He hasn't had a chance to talk to ya, and from Jersey City, your good friend, Bubani Umbazo. He started his car, he started his car, with your album on . . . and now he's a highway.

There's a sound guideline in stand-up comedy that you have an expansive license to ridicule everything you are. If you're Catholic you can put down your Catholic upbringing; if you're gay you can put down gays; if you're Asian you can put down Asians; if you're overweight you can put down overweight people; and so on. But that license shrinks drastically when the subject of your put-down jokes has to do with people and things you are not. You're in treacherous waters if you're Jewish and you put down Catholicism, or if you're straight and you put down gays, and so on.

Successful put-down comedians like Rickles ignore this guideline. They put down everyone. They get away with it because their jokes are never personal. If an Asian member of his audience had a disability, Rickles would never make jokes about the disability. His jokes would center on impersonal Asian stereotypes. The only people Rickles would put down for their looks were actually attractive. He made it clear that behind the insults were respect and affection. At the end of a Rickles performance, he'd articulate these feelings. Here's how he concluded a Sinatra roast:

> This wonderful gentleman that we honor tonight was in my corner then, he's in my corner now. We do not dance together; we do not break bread every day together. But when I'm in his company, Dean [Martin] knows this and you know this, I speak of him with love. And I tell ya, we have been blessed to have such a man. Goodnight.

Underneath Mr. Warmth . . . was Mr. Warmth.

Lisa Lampanelli is her generation's leading insult comedian, which has earned her the moniker "the Queen of Mean." Her act is cruder than Rickles's and, also unlike him, she works dirty. But she adheres to the essential principles of insult comedy: Her jokes come from a place of fun (in her case, naughty fun) and not a place of venom and hostility. Her jokes embody salient racial, ethnic, gender, sexual, and religious stereotyping—but they are never personal.

Here's a sampling of the jokes she performed in Joliet, Illinois. You need to know she was performing in Joliet to get her opening joke, which insults all the women in her audience.

> Oh my God, look at you people! Joliet! You guys, you are not as ugly <u>as I thought you'd be</u>. No seriously, look at all the women, how beautiful. <u>They're like Joliet 10s, New York 3s, but who's counting?</u> That's OK. You're so cute. Look at every

type of person. Blacks. <u>Blacks!</u> Right in the front, <u>how did this</u> <u>happen.</u> You people win one election and <u>see, look at this!</u> . . .
. . . Oh! I can tell by your Flock of Seagulls haircuts, <u>there's two</u> <u>lesbians here. Wowww!</u> Now are you girls, hey, <u>are you les-beans?</u> Wow, why aren't you out <u>building a Habitat for Humanity house?</u> Isn't that cute. And look in the front row. Identifiable, <u>Jew and not-</u> <u>Jew.</u> So I'm assuming only <u>one of you has a small penis. I mean her.</u>

When this performance was videoed, the shot would cut from Lampanelli to the people she was insulting. In every case, their reaction was delight. No feelings were being hurt by these jokes because they weren't personal. They were targeted strictly at impersonal stereotypes, and delivered without a trace of malice

The fans of insult comedians like Don Rickles and Lisa Lampanelli go to see them to hear politically incorrect insults and perhaps even to be insulted themselves. Such acts are comedic safety valves that release racial, ethnic, regional, national, religious, and gender prejudices in a way that brings people together rather than tearing them apart. Insult comedians comically stand up for democracy by affirming that *all* people—no matter their race, sex, creed, or color—have something wrong with them. It's the democratic spirit of insult comedians that makes them funny. It would be disastrous for an insult comedian to single out one group of people to ridicule. That would be bigotry. Bigotry is not funny; it's loathsome.

It would also be disastrous for a comedian to do jokes that are personally insulting to an innocent audience member. When I was in high school, I took my girlfriend to the Peppermint Lounge in New York to see an insult comedian, thinking it would be a fun evening. This guy performed holding a flashlight. He'd point it at someone in the audience and then insult the way that person actually looked. I still remember the firm grasp of my girlfriend's hand as she restrained me from getting up and punching this guy when he shone his flashlight in my face and made fun of my large nose. This wasn't a comedian. This was a mean-spirited SOB. I'm not leaving out his name to protect him.

I can't remember his name. He and his flashlight have justly sunk into comedy oblivion.

For most comedians, insult comedy isn't their entire act. It's a spice rather than the main course. This is the case with Jackie Mason. Mason is a masterful comedian. Everything he does, he does superbly. And that includes insulting his audience. It's the way he usually opens his act. One of his techniques is to ask what sounds like a rhetorical question, and then get annoyed when an audience member doesn't answer it. On the opening night of his show in Toronto, the microphone malfunctioned and people in the balcony couldn't hear him. He handled the situation with comedic aplomb:

> You still can't hear me back there? (Yeses and noes from the audience.) Maybe I can go from person to person and do the show. . . . How come you people keep laughing if you say you can't hear me? Who are you laughing at if you can't hear me? (Addressing a person in the first row) Answer this question or get the hell out of here!

It's part of Mason's strategy to pick on people who are completely innocent of any wrongdoing. In the Toronto performance, Mason didn't insult someone in the balcony who might have said he couldn't hear but still laughed at the jokes. Instead, he insulted someone in the first row who obviously had no trouble hearing at all. Not only does the punishment inflicted by a Mason insult not fit any audience member's crime—there *is* no crime. It's the randomness and inappropriateness of his insult jokes that make them funny.

Here's how he opened his Broadway show *The World According to Me*:

> You see, this show is not for everybody. I don't know if you noticed it. (To an audience member) I realized it as soon as you came in here, Mister.

The only prerequisite for being on the receiving end of a Mason insult is the obviousness of your innocence. In act 2 of his Broadway

show, the set was a full-stage map of the world. He began this act by
insulting whole sections of his audience:

> First of all, this is a map of the world. I explain it to you because
> I can see there are people here who have no idea of what's going
> on. . . . The main problem of the world today is hate. There is more
> hate all over the world today than ever before. Hate is the main
> problem and it's all over the world. A lot of people think (point-
> ing to the right side of the audience) that it's just in this section.

To create your own insult jokes it's useful to think of the common, innocent things that go on in the audience when you're performing. During your set, for example, latecomers may arrive. When
this happens to the comedian Clayton Fletcher, he has this to say:

> Wow, we have some lovely people coming in a little late.
> (Addressing latecomers) Welcome. Can I get you something?
> A menu? A waiter? A watch?!

If someone is texting during your act, say something like:

> *Oh, you're texting. OMG, FYI, not cool. Angry Cat Emoji.*

And so on.

Insult jokes work effectively with other forms of stand-up, or as an
entire act, when they're delivered in a context that includes the following:

- A sense of warmth and fun coming from the comedian, as
  opposed to anger and hostility
- A democratic spirit in the jokes that sends the message that
  there is something wrong with every group of people, not just
  one or a few
- Jokes that aren't personal and hurtful

Got that, you hockey puck?

12

PUT-DOWN HUMOR — SELF-DEPRECATING HUMOR

SELF-DEPRECATING HUMOR is a particularly endearing form of stand-up. There's something likable and liberating about someone who freely acknowledges his or her shortcomings. Most of us are disappointed by some aspect of ourselves. But usually we don't want to talk about it, because we don't feel good about it; it's not something we want to share with others. Sometimes we don't want to talk about it because we don't want to admit to ourselves that this shortcoming exists, even though we know it does: *I know there's a lot of hair in the drain after I shampoo but THAT DOESN'T MEAN I'M GOING BALD! DAMN IT!*

Comedy is a forum for unvarnished truth. It's a place where we can openly and publicly face our weaknesses, imperfections, and fears. The comedian holds these things up for ridicule and we, in the audience, recognize these foibles in ourselves and laugh at them. Our laughter cuts these anxiety-producing shortcomings down to size. They no longer overwhelm us. The message behind the comedian's self-deprecating jokes is, *Yeah, I'm going bald [I'm short, I'm flat-chested, I'm fat, I'm single, etc., etc., etc.], but so are other people in this room and we can laugh about it. So we're OK. HAH!*

When stand-ups put themselves down for shortcomings that are widely shared by their audience, big laughs are often the result. Here's a good example from a piece by Laura Bassi, a new comedian and student of mine. In this piece she puts herself down for being a single college graduate in her mid-20s whose career is babysitting. Being drastically underemployed is a predicament shared by many young people who haven't figured out what they want to do with their lives. Laura gets big laughs with this material, in part, because her audiences see her struggle as their own:

> So I babysit, as a job. (Pause.) Thank you for just staring at me, it makes me feel like I'm telling <u>my parents that again</u>. But it's fine. I'm just trying to figure it out. I mean, I just graduated college. <u>Five years ago.</u> The moms love me, though. They're like, **"<u>You're so available!</u> All our other sitters have parties and formals and all these social gatherings"**—I'm like **"OK, YEAH! <u>I get it. Got it. Thanks.</u>"** My favorite age to babysit are infants, because they're amused by anything you say, as long as you use the right inflection. So I just use it as a therapy session. And I'll be like, (in baby-talk voice) **"HEY! Six more people got <u>engaged on Facebook today!</u> (Makes her hand <u>into a gun and shoots at her head</u>) Pshew! And Justin and Leah bought a house! I live in . . . a hallway! My door is <u>a shower curtain</u>! And if I have to buy one more bridesmaid's dress, I'm going to check myself <u>into a mental institution!</u> I'll be <u>strapped down like you!</u> And I'm never getting married because I hate men. I hate them, <u>they all suck</u>, I hate them I hate them I hate them <u>I hate them—OK.</u>"**

Ultimately, what gives an audience the license to laugh at your problems is a clear signal from you that you're OK with them. If they feel you're devastated by your problems, the audience can't laugh. It would be mean, unthinkable. And what signals the audience that you're OK with your problems is the fact that you are performing comedy about them. If you find them funny, so can we. We can see comedy in Laura Bassi's babysitting "career" and her trouble with men because she can. We couldn't laugh, otherwise.

Often, the target of self-deprecating humor are the comedian's looks. Phyllis Diller, whose put-down jokes about her husband are quoted in chapter 9, was most famous for putting down her looks, sex appeal (or lack thereof), and flamboyant wardrobe:

> You think I'm overdressed, this is my slip. I got a figure that just won't start. My body is in such bad shape, I wear prescription underwear. I finally had a ship tattooed on my chest; I wanted something on it. Would you believe that I once entered a beauty contest? I must have been out of my mind. I not only came in last, I got 361 "get well" cards. I don't want you to get the idea that I have given up on my looks. I will never give up. I am in my fourteenth year of a ten-day beauty plan. When I go to bed at night, I've got so much grease on my body I wear snow chains to hold up my gown. We've got more grease stains in the bedroom than we've got in the garage. One night I asked Fang to kiss me goodnight, he got up and put on his work clothes. You know the lights have gone out with dirty old Fang: the last time there was a gleam in Fang's eye, there was a short in his electric blanket.

On the page, Phyllis Diller's jokes seem to be old-school one-liners that feed negative stereotypes of what a woman should be. But the generation of women comedians that followed her—Roseanne and Ellen DeGeneres, for example—looked up to her as a role model and inspiration. These are women whose comedy was infused with feminism. *Why did they look up to her?* you may wonder. That's a good question.

Here's the answer. Phyllis Diller came up in the comedy scene during the 1950s, a time when being conventional was looked upon as a great attribute. She was virtually the only woman headliner on the circuit. The very fact that she was performing stand-up was unconventional. She created a persona that was the polar opposite of the era's conventional *Leave It to Beaver* housewife. Her hair looked like someone had just set off a firecracker in it. Her outfits looked like they'd been designed by the Barnum & Bailey Circus. And, famously, her response to the shortcomings of her looks, sex appeal, and marriage was a loud, outrageous laugh.

Phyllis Diller achieved what all great comedians achieve: she found her story. Her story was, *I'm an oddball. I'm not hiding it. I'm putting it in your face. I don't fit in at all and I find that absolutely hilarious.* Her story resonated with feminists, gays, and other people who did not feel at home in the '50s and early '60s. In her time Phyllis Diller was not old-school. She was totally out of the box.

Sometimes new comedians shy away from self-deprecating humor because they feel it makes them out to be victims. In comedy, this is never true. It can't be true. Comedy ends happily. The comedian is not overwhelmed by his struggles. That's the stuff of tragedy, not comedy. The spirit of the comedian is vulnerable but indestructible. The comedian looks unblinkingly at his or her shortcomings and utilizes them not to create sympathy or pity, but to create laughter. That's not the mindset of a victim. It's the mindset of a hero.

This brings us to Richard Pryor. To a degree unmatched before or since, Richard Pryor created comedy out of his fear and pain. A subject of one of his great sets, *Live on the Sunset Strip*, was his near-fatal drug addiction. He set himself on fire freebasing cocaine. Out of this nightmare, he made comedy.

At the end of his life, he was crippled and nearly blind from MS. There were persistent rumors that he had died. Seated onstage in a chair because he was unable to stand or clearly see, he performed stand-up about this final stage of his life:

(Audience member shouts, "Richard, you ain't dead!") Wait a minute. Of course I'm not dead! Wait a minute. No. <u>I'm not dead!</u> 'Cause sometimes they used to have that on the <u>news and shit, that I was dead.</u> You know, it's a bitch if you be <u>watchin' the news,</u> and a motherfucker <u>be talking about you dead.</u> And my <u>accountant called me up, talking about,</u> **"Oh, I thought you**

were dead." I said, **"Well, I'm not dead. I wanna check the books too."** That's to me, is the weirdest shit is to be assumed dead <u>but you still be alive</u>. And people come in your house, like the housekeeper and shit, they come in and see you sleeping and if you don't say nothing <u>they get scared</u>. And they make a lot of noise. **"RICHAAAARRRDDDDD!!!!!"** **"Yeess?"** <u>"Oh, it's all right, I thought you were dead."</u>

Pryor goes on to say that the disease has rendered him incontinent, impotent, and unable to stop his arms from flailing about. Stuck in a car in an L.A. traffic jam, with cars at a standstill in both directions, he's approached by an attractive woman who recognizes him. She starts talking to him, he's attracted to her, and meanwhile he's peeing in his pants and his arms are flying around uncontrollably:

You know, <u>it's a bitch when your bladder and your arm turn against you</u>. And she's standing there, and I'm looking, **<u>"Hiiii."</u>** **"Oh, you so funny, stop waving."** I smiled. And I'm thinking, **"I'd like to fuck her!"** And my dick's sayin', <u>"Try."</u> So, you know, you go through it, it does something to your muscles. Neurologists say it does something to the muscles. It's a funny disease. I guess it's God's way of saying, <u>"You've already fucked all you gonna."</u>

The audience could see and hear that Richard Pryor did not have long to live. In that sense he was not OK. His farewell at the end of this performance was clearly a final farewell:

If you could see what I see today, as I look out there at ya's . . . I see the peoples, and all the beautiful colors. They're so beautiful. And it makes me so happy. God bless all you all . . . I'm outta here!

What was abundantly clear to his audience was that seated onstage was a comedian who looked squarely at his imminent death and laughed at it. He was slashing terminal illness down to size. Yeah, Richard was going out, but he was going out with laughter. If he could laugh, we could laugh. Dying, Richard Pryor was OK.

On display in this chapter's excerpts are three totally different styles of self-deprecating humor spanning 60 years. Styles change. But the forms endure. I make this point because I don't want you to confuse forms and content. The content is ever changing. It's about you and the times in which you live. The forms are always there to inspire you and to give shape to your comic ideas, just as they did for your forefathers and foremothers in comedy.

13

CROWD WORK

WHEN A COMEDIAN INVITES A MEMBER or members of the audience to engage with him in a back-and-forth conversation, that is called "crowd work." It's a form of stand-up that, in addition to being entertaining, is enormously useful in a variety of specific circumstances you'll encounter as a comedian.

The first road gig you're likely to get will call on you to be the opening act and master of ceremonies (MC) for the show. Crowd work is part of an MC's skill set. Successful crowd work at the opening of the show can stop the audience from talking among themselves and get them focused on the MC. The conversation moves from the audience to the stage. People have to pay attention to the person in the spotlight when that person is talking directly to them.

Wherever you're placed in the show's lineup, crowd work is a move to make when you feel your jokes aren't scoring with the audience. I'm not talking about a joke or two not working. That's fine. If most of the jokes are working, just continue on with your set. I'm talking about a situation where you're opening your set with your "A" jokes (the ones that usually get the biggest laughs) and you're out there for a minute or so and nothing is working. You're on the verge of bombing. In my chapter on bombing, I'll give you a detailed strategy for successfully handling this most dreaded situation. But I bring up bombing in this chapter too because it's a circumstance where crowd work can work wonders. It's a potent way to get an audience that isn't laughing—and therefore not paying much attention to you—to refocus on you and start laughing at your jokes. As an audience member you can ignore someone onstage who is telling jokes that aren't that funny to you. But you can't ignore the comedian when he starts talking directly to you and is engaging you in conversation.

Crowd work can also serve as a comedic Hamburger Helper when you need to stretch your time onstage. For instance, say you're the opening act and it's showtime and the featured act hasn't shown up. The club manager looks at you with desperation and tells you to stretch your act. But all the material you've got is already in your set. It's crowd-work time!

In addition to helping you MC, and helping you deal with a tough audience, and enabling you to add time to your set, crowd work is a form of stand-up that can be an entertaining part of your set under any circumstances.

Much of crowd work is written. (Shhh! Now that you have joined the fellowship of comedians, that trade secret has got to stay between us.) It can also be ad-libbed. Often it's both. A comedian who enjoys improvising can have some solid crowd-work jokes prepared and use them along with ad-libbed remarks.

Whether crowd work is written or improvised, it's done in four clearly defined steps.

Step one is to ask a simple question that can be answered easily in a word or two. Many people in the audience don't want to be seated close to the stage because they don't want to be picked on by the comedians. They get flustered at the thought of suddenly becoming part of the show. When you do crowd work you need people to engage with you in conversation, so you want to make it simple and easy for them to participate. So don't ask, "Do you see the growing criticism of a traditional liberal arts education as a waste of time and money, and the rejection of science among climate change deniers, and the rise of the extreme right in Europe and the US as the coming of a new dark age; or do you see it as just part of the usual course of human events?" It's better to ask, "So where are you from?"

Another reason to ask questions that can be answered in a word or two, and without much thought, is that it saves time. You don't want an audience member dominating your stage time by giving long answers to your questions.

The second step in crowd work is to observe and listen to the person answering your question. You want your response to key off what they just said, or how they said it, or how they look, or whom they're sitting with. You want to work with what your conversation partners are offering you. The more closely you observe and listen to them, the wider will be your range of possible funny responses.

The third step is the hardest. It's to repeat or paraphrase the audience member's response to your question. You need to do this because you're the only one with the microphone. Your response is going to key off what the audience member said; so to be sure that everyone in the audience heard what was said, you need to repeat or paraphrase it. That's the hardest step in crowd work, because it's the only one that is counterintuitive. The other steps involve doing what you do naturally when you're talking with someone. You talk, you listen, you reply. Repeating or paraphrasing what the other person said does not come naturally, so at first it will require concentration to do it. Like riding a bike, however, after a while you'll get used to it and it will come naturally.

The fourth step in crowd work is to respond to the audience member's answer or to something specific you've observed about him or her. You can, if you wish, continue the conversation by repeating these four steps.

Moshe Kasher is a comedian whose act prominently features crowd work. We can break down this excerpt from his act into the four steps.

1. Ask a simple question that can easily be answered in a word or two. *(To a group of four young women) So how old are you guys?*

2. Listen to the reply.
3. Repeat or paraphrase the answer. *You guys are twenty.*
4. Respond. *(Sweetly) Ah, you haven't done anything.*

Crowd work can be as carefully written and honed as any part of your set. But the audience, bless their souls, thinks it is ad-libbed. *That hysterical thing the comedian just said couldn't have been planned. How could he have known what that person in the audience would say to him?* The comedian *can* know what the person in the audience will say. If, for example, he asks a yes or no question, he can write a joke to respond to yes, and a joke to respond to no. The key to writing crowd work is asking questions to which you can determine the range of answers, and then writing jokes that are set up by those answers. Written crowd work is accomplished by letting someone in the audience do the setup to your joke and then you delivering your written punchline.

The biggest laughs you get onstage happen when the audience thinks you're being spontaneously funny. Written crowd work creates the illusion of spontaneity, and for that reason can be a high point of your set. Further, you can expand the illusion of spontaneity into your written non-crowd-work set pieces by introducing them with crowd work. It can appear that you're riffing on something introduced by chance just a moment before by a member of your audience.

For an example of written crowd work, let's look at a piece once performed by Mary Dimino, winner of a MAC Award for Best Female Stand-Up and a former student of mine. Something you could never guess from seeing Mary now is that, at the very beginning of her career, she was morbidly obese. It was a condition that was so "out there" that she had to address it in her act in order to get on to other subjects. Mary and I decided to address it with written crowd work. Here is how it went:

1. Ask a simple question. *(To a man in the first row, sweetly and sincerely) Sir, it's your honesty that I'm looking for here. Do you think I'm fat?*

2. Listen and observe.

Now, we knew that the answer to that question was going to be a yes or a no. If it was a no, here is how the joke played out.

3. Repeat or paraphrase. _No!_
4. Respond. _You are so sweet! (Mary sits on the man's lap and continues her monologue.)_

If the reply was a yes, it played out this way.

3. Repeat or paraphrase. _Yes!_
4. Respond. _(Furious) You son of a bitch. You think you can just walk in here and call me fat. You bastard!_

It's possible to get laughs at every step in crowd work. Asking the question can get a laugh. Mary asking for an honest answer to the question "Do you think I'm fat?" always got laughs because the answer was so abundantly obvious. She also got laughs on her listening because she did it with a totally unwarranted facial expression of hopeful optimism. She looked like a kid about to open up what she believes to be a fabulous present. Her repeating the answer got laughs too: she melted with flirtatious affection when she repeated a "no"; she erupted with volcanic outrage when she repeated a "yes"—it was hilarious that she was shocked and outraged when a person gave the only possible honest answer to her question. The written fourth steps also became big, reliable "A" laughs.

For comedians who are good at improvising, crowd work is a form of stand-up that enables them to exercise that gift. Joan Keiter, now a writer living in London, started her career as a stand-up in New York. Her persona was that of a very hip, angry Lower East Sider—a New York bohemian always coolly dressed in black. I was working on crowd work with Joan, and gave her an in-performance exercise to do: a five-minute set with three minutes of written material interspersed with two minutes of ad-libbed crowd work using the four steps. She opened her crowd work by asking a man in the first row some innocuous question like, "Where are you from?" While the man was replying, Joan observed that he was wearing a completely out-of-fashion '50s-style French beret. When Joan got to step three, rather than paraphrasing what the man said, she told the audience what she'd observed about him. She described his hat so everyone in the audience would know what she was looking at:

3. *Sir, I see you are wearing a French beret.*
4. *Are you doing that just to annoy me or are you trying to annoy the whole audience?*

Big laugh.

A cool thing about improvised crowd work is that sometimes, after you've performed your set, you'll think of a great rejoinder to an audience member's answer that you didn't come up with that night onstage. In "real life," of course, you don't get a second chance to use the witty comeback you thought of only *after* you left the party or meeting where you wish you'd said it. With crowd work you always have that opportunity. Come up with a great comeback, far better than the one you ad-libbed, then put it in your next show.

There's one caveat concerning crowd work. If you're auditioning for a spot on a late-night talk show like *The Tonight Show* or *The Late Show*, it's best not to include crowd work in the audition set. First, it's awkward to get camera coverage of both you and the audience member you choose to work with. Second, these shows need to know, down to the second, how long your set is. It's just about impossible to time crowd work down to the second, because the audience member's response to your question is something of a wild card. If you phrased the question right, the answer should be brief, but you can't count on that. Further, anything ad-libbed in your set runs a higher risk of failure than material that has proven to be funny over and over again in performance. A brilliantly talented student of mine got an audition for *The Tonight Show*. For the audition, the producers watched her perform at the Improv in L.A. Sadly and foolishly, she chose to do wall-to-wall crowd work that night. The feedback was that her audition gave the producers no idea of what she'd do on the show. And that was the end of that. When the stakes are high, go with your tried-and-true material.

With that warning label on the crowd-work package, start smokin'.

14

THE COMIC FLAW

CHEAP, DITZY, GROSS, NEUROTIC, INSENSITIVE, self-centered, bigoted, confused, a jerk—these words describe human shortcomings. When a comedian creates a persona that embodies a shortcoming, this form of stand-up comedy is called the *comic flaw*.

There are two keys to creating this form of stand-up. The comic flaw comedian must not be aware of his or her flaw. The cheap person doesn't know he's cheap, the dumb person doesn't know he's dumb, and so on. We know it, but they don't. Amy Schumer's stand-up material can be gross, like her jokes about how her unwashed panties look. But she knows she's being gross, so those are not comic flaw jokes.

The second key is that if the shortcoming is a malicious one like bigotry, it must be clear in the writing that it's being held up for ridicule. It's there to be laughed at, not taken as a valid, albeit controversial, point of view. Otherwise, the audience will detest the comedian.

Sarah Silverman is one of her generation's most skilled comic flaw comedians. Her persona is that of a blatantly bigoted and insensitive person who is so unaware of those flaws that she's hilariously mystified and offended when confronted with them:

I used to go out with a guy who is half black who totally broke up with me because <u>I'm a fucking loser and, um</u>—I just heard

myself say that, I'm such a pessimist, I have the worst attitude—he's half white. And he totally broke up with me. And
it's funny now, like, what is it, hindsight's 20/20 or whatever.
It's so obvious to me now, why he broke up with me. Because
he has fucking low self-esteem. You know? And I can't compete with that. Like everybody knows somebody who, it's like
anything you say to them, they're gonna take it, they're gonna
hear it in the most negative way. You know what I mean? And
he was like, you could give him a comp—like, I gave him a
compliment, all right? I told him he probably would have made
like a really expensive slave. Like in the olden timey days. Not
now. And what does he do, right? It goes through the uh, Rube
Goldberg crazy straw of his low self-esteem, and it hit his ear
and he heard something fucked up. I can't control that. I can't
control what he hears, you know. He has to learn how to love
himself. Before I can stop hating his people. As a people.

Silverman's delivery of these jokes, including her look of absolute
cluelessness, makes it clear that she and her bigotry are what we've
been invited to laugh at. If there were the slightest implication that
these views were to be taken as the valid opinions of a thoughtful
person, we'd be too busy hating her to laugh.

Comic flaw comedians have two guns in their comedy arsenal:
they can get audiences to laugh both *with* them and *at* them. Such is
the case with a student of mine, the actor and stand-up Kate Redway.
Her flaw is a benign one: she's confused about things that most people
take for granted. In her confusion Kate stumbles into real insights:

I don't go to church anymore because all they read is the Bible
and I already read that. Besides, there is stuff in the Bible I
just don't get.

     Like why did God have only one son? Was Jesus such a
handful that God was like, "Whoa, one is enough!" The Bible
doesn't say that Jesus was a problem child. Besides, Mary did
all the work. Talk about marriage inequality. It was like God

was everywhere except helping her out in the house. And let's face it: God was not the most attentive father. He hardly ever spoke to Jesus. He spoke to Moses all the time. "I'm over here in this bush." "Write down these ten things." I think in his entire life Jesus asked God only one question: "Why hast Thou forsaken me?" And God didn't answer that. And that was a damn good question.

Steve Martin, a comic flaw comedian, is one of the most successful stand-ups of all time. He quit performing stand-up in 1981, for the same reason the Beatles stopped giving live concerts in 1966: he couldn't be heard even with a powerful stadium sound system, because his adoring fans screamed throughout his entire set. This fan mania ended a wildly successful stand-up career.

Martin's stand-up persona was a parody of the all-around show-biz performer. He did everything: he was a comic, an impressionist, a magician, dancer, singer. Hilariously, he stunk at it all. His jokes often had no apparent punchlines. His impressions reminded you of no one other than him; when he danced it looked like he was being electrocuted. When he performed magic either nothing happened or something would happen and he would lose control of it. When he made balloon animals, not only didn't they look like animals, they were so misshapen they didn't even look like balloons. He was ecstatically oblivious to his ineptitude. He clearly saw himself as the suavest, swingingest, sexiest, coolest, wildest performer to ever set foot onstage. That was his comic flaw.

Here is Martin doing stand-up on how he meets girls:

This is the way I meet girls. By looking cool. The important thing is to have a great opening line, you gotta have the drink, you go up to the girl and you go: (He "suavely" drinks from his glass of water, takes a few casual steps toward the girl.) Yeah, I make a lot of money. (Takes another sip of his drink, savors it.) I'm in the stock market. (Huge self-satisfied smile.) I don't know if you know anything about the STOCK market or not but, uh, if you do you'll appreciate this . . . <u>I bought</u> <u>cardboard when it was 14 cents a ton.</u> (Very impressed with himself, he takes another sip of his drink, savors it.) <u>And it's</u> <u>up to 16 cents now, so</u> . . . (Incredibly impressed with himself.) And I bought three tons of it, <u>so let's see</u> . . . (he closes his eyes and tries to do the math. Long pause. Takes another sip of his drink.) Well, you figure it out. Yeah, I just got me a new car, though, so I'm pretty proud of it. (Big smirky smile.) And you know how it is when you get a new car, you can't wait to get out there and . . . it's a prestige car: '65 Greyhound bus. Well, I put a lot of money into it, you know, <u>I put a new dog on the</u> <u>side.</u> Greatest thing about it, you know, BESIDES being able to get <u>up to thirty tons of luggage in it</u>, you take a girl out and you say, "Hey want to get in the backseat?" and <u>you got, like,</u> <u>thirty chances.</u>

Steve Martin's persona was a comic archetype—the jerk. He was his generation's most successful. (The first movie that he cowrote and starred in was titled *The Jerk.*) Jerry Lewis was his generation's great jerk. Larry David in *Curb Your Enthusiasm* is the great jerk of the new millennium. Things that might annoy us slightly and temporarily, he obsesses about. He globalizes the trivial. He makes much ado about nothing. He won't let things go. He's like a dog with a bone in his mouth. He's a pain in the ass. And we love him.

Audiences often love comedians who master the comic flaw—in part because their vulnerability is so out there. They make no attempt to disguise their flaw because they don't know they have it. This creates a persona that is so very human and identifiable. *Oh my God,* *he's never happy with where he's seated in a restaurant. That's just* *like my Uncle Charlie!* Audiences also enjoy feeling superior to flawed comedians: we know them way better than they know themselves.

If you find yourself heading in the direction of comic flaw stand-up, keep going. You are on a golden road.

15

CHARACTER STAND-UP COMEDY

A STAND-UP WHOSE PERSONA IS OBVIOUSLY FANCIFUL is performing *character stand-up*. This form is different from act-outs. When Richard Pryor enacted other characters in a story, it was Richard acting out the mobster club owner or Richard acting out the football player Jim Brown. Gilbert Gottfried, on the other hand, is always the fictional character he has created. Every time he performs, he's this character. When he's a guest on a talk show, he's this character. When he's a voice actor in a movie or commercial, his voice is the voice of this character. His whole career is performing this character. That is character stand-up comedy. The audience knows that these characters exist only onstage. The stage persona bears no resemblance to any real person. He or she is a made-up character, clearly. Pee-wee Herman, Steve Martin, Jackie "Moms" Mabley, and sometimes (as I'll explain) Andy Kaufman are also comedians who exemplify this form of stand-up.

You can get a good if incomplete picture of most stand-ups' routines by reading their material. Their stage personas and their emotional lives are vividly present in the words they say onstage. This is far less the case with character stand-up. This form is achieved principally through physical means: how the comedians look, what they're wearing, their haircut, the way they sound, what they're doing onstage. It is less what they say than how they say it.

What comes out of Gilbert Gottfried's mouth are intentionally generic, old-fashioned, often dirty jokes:

> A landlord is showing a couple around an apartment. The husband looks up and says, "Wait a minute. This apartment doesn't have a ceiling." The landlord answers, "That's OK. The people upstairs don't walk around that much."

If you only knew Gilbert Gottfried from reading his jokes, you'd think he was a hack. He's not. He's original and funny. What makes him so is the character he has created. He doesn't talk to us, he yells at us. He doesn't look at us, he squints at us as if the sight of us hurts his eyes. He's belligerent. We annoy him. It's our fault that he has to shout his jokes, because if he didn't we'd be unable to get them. The lamer his jokes are, the more we laugh at the exhausting effort he expends on telling them.

Pee-wee Herman is a childlike character created by Paul Reubens. His signature retort, "I know you are but what am I?" is the language of an elementary-school playground circa the 1950s. His act is a combination of character comedy and prop comedy. Prop comedy is a form of stand-up where the jokes are keyed off objects. So, for a Halloween appearance on Letterman, he came out in a devil costume, reached into a bag, and pulled out a little girl's blue dress. Letterman looked at him quizzically, and Pee-wee explained, "Devil with the blue dress," which is the lyric to a classic rock 'n' roll song. As with Gilbert Gottfried, Pee-wee's jokes are intentionally lame. His comedy resides not in his words but in his character. This cartoonish, childlike man in his gray suit and red bow tie—who sometimes wears lipstick, who speaks in a high-pitched childish voice and has a maniacal laugh, and who can, in his childlike way, be sweet one minute and a brat the next—carries with him a bag of toys, costume pieces, gag gifts, and other props. He tells jokes about these things. More important, like a child, he creates his own worlds out of these things and, like a child, he enters fully into these imaginary worlds and they become his playhouse. He invites us in to play with him. But like the child who owns the ball, he makes it clear that he makes the rules. He may act silly and childish but he's in charge. His act goes beyond telling jokes. It's an opportunity for us to accompany Pee-wee back to childhood. Fun.

Andy Kaufman was a master of character comedy. At least I'm pretty sure he was. I'm qualifying this because, more than any other comedian, Andy Kaufman blurred the line between what is real and what is an act. At times, you couldn't tell whether he was performing comedy or whether something real and unsettling was happening. The producers of *Saturday Night Live* couldn't tell when Kaufman screen-tested for the show. After a hesitant, stumbling start he gave a very sincere recitation of the lyrics to "MacArthur Park," a pop song that was known for its sappy and pretentious lyrics. Here is the chorus:

> *Someone left the cake out in the rain*
> *I don't think that I can take it*
> *'Cause it took so long to make it*
> *And I'll never have that recipe again*

Reciting these insipid lyrics, Kaufman looked like he was moved to his very core. When he finished he had a triumphant, almost childlike smile on his face. He didn't say anything, but it looked like he was thinking, *I did it! Did you like it?!* The person conducting the audition couldn't tell if this was a comedy performance or a strange dude who somehow got an audition and had no idea that what he'd just performed was unintentionally hilarious. He asked Kaufman to do it again. Kaufman asked, "The same way?" "Exactly the same, if you can," was the reply. Kaufman proceeded to give the exact same performance, including the exact same stumbling start. His entire audition—not just when he was "performing" the lyric but also when he was supposedly not performing and just talking with the audition auditors—was an act.

Kaufman created a character who was anxious and insecure but who, most of the time, was able to summon up the courage to perform. He made performing comedy an existential struggle to survive. In his legendary performance on the first episode of *Saturday Night Live*, he lip-synched the *Mighty Mouse* theme song. Specifically, he lip-synched the part of the song that goes, "Here I come to save the day"—which occurs only twice in a song that is nearly two minutes long. For most of the song, then, he stood anxiously and waited to come in for his small part. His hands were tense. They twitched nervously. His face was grim with concentration. He looked like a man who knew that if he was not super careful he could totally screw up. He could come in too soon, or not come in when he should. He could fail. Complete failure was a very real possibility. He looked like he was staring right at it. When it was time to lip-synch his line, he gave it his all, transforming into the super-confident superhero Mighty Mouse. When he finished the phrase, his anxiety instantly returned as he concentrated on when to come in next. These abrupt transformations from the anxious performer, Andy, to the confident character he was performing, Mighty Mouse, were hilarious and were greeted with gales of laughter. Andy Kaufman turned lip-synching a cartoon theme song being played on a cheap portable record player into a life-and-death situation. When he made it through, the audience went wild. He survived!

Kaufman used character comedy to create seemingly awkward situations that were in fact extended pranks. The laughs came from seeing how he, or whomever he was sharing the stage with, or his audience, coped with his awkwardness. His awkwardness was the setup; how it was coped with was the punch. An example of this occurred on David Letterman's morning show. Kaufman comes out. He looks nervous. He shakes Dave's hand, sits, and his nose is running. He rubs his nose, but it keeps running. We can clearly see it running in close-ups. Dave tries to interview him, but Andy's nose keeps running and he seems too distressed to do anything about it. The studio audience laughs. He looks at them fearfully: *Why are they laughing?* This was part of Kaufman's persona: he didn't understand why people laughed when he was being "sincere." Dave has to do something—he can't have a guest with mucus streaming out of his nose. He offers Andy a Kleenex, and it looks like the awkwardness is over. But it's just starting.

The guest interview on a talk show is a format for the guests to promote their latest projects. So, with the nose situation seemingly under control, Dave asks Andy about his upcoming projects. Andy says he doesn't have any. Now there's nothing to talk about. Dave breaks the awkward silence by inviting Andy to perform the "little something" he's prepared. Andy moves from the guest chair to the performance area of the stage. He begins with a long, sincere, somber, laugh-free expression of thanks to Dave for having him on the show. His nose isn't running anymore—but he's started to cough.

The audience laughs. He looks at them puzzled and hurt. Andy proceeds to tell them, through his coughs, that he has no work and that his wife has left him and taken his two children and his money. The audience laughs. Andy asks them not to.

So now his anxiety has put Dave in the awkward position of having a talk show guest with nothing to say, and it has put Dave's studio audience in the awkward position of not knowing whether or not they should laugh. Is this a funny bit or is this real and sad?

Then Andy asks the studio audience for money. People start actually giving him some until he's escorted out of the studio by security. Not a single funny word has been spoken, but the laughs—except when Andy asked for the audience not to laugh and they thought he was being serious—have been nonstop.

That is character comedy. Kaufman's act wasn't composed of jokes. It was composed of pranks that challenged whoever witnessed his performances—whether it was an audience or the professionals he worked with—to distinguish illusion from reality.

Kaufman sometimes appeared as another character: Tony Clifton, a sleazy Vegas lounge performer whose misogyny was so blatant he'd get into physical altercations with women in his audience. A prank. But despite having played two characters rather than one, Kaufman still qualifies as a character comedian. The reason is that he refused to admit that he *was* Tony Clifton. In real life, for instance, he made his manager, George Shapiro, negotiate a separate contract for Tony Clifton to appear on several episodes of Kaufman's sitcom *Taxi*. Kaufman pranked onstage and off. He was a comedian for whom "all the world's a stage."

To some degree, all successful comedians create who they are behind the microphone. Sometimes their creations are drawn from aspects of their offstage selves. And sometimes, as in character comedy, they're entirely works of fiction. As long as you get consistent laughs, you, behind the microphone, can be anyone you want to be. How cool is that?

16

EDGY STAND-UP COMEDY

WHEN A STAND-UP SPEAKS THE UNSPEAKABLE, talks about subjects one shouldn't discuss, sometimes using language that's considered unacceptable in civil society, that is "edgy" stand-up. Edgy stand-up is aspired to by legions of comedians, but is becoming harder and harder to achieve. Here's the reason: We live in an era of "anything goes." What's unspeakable anymore?

Sex used to be a taboo subject. In 1927 the Broadway play *Sex*, written by and starring the great comedian and comedy writer Mae West, was raided by the New York City Police Department. The play contained no nudity or curse words. No sexual acts were performed or simulated. The fact that the play's title was *Sex*, and that its cast of characters included prostitutes and pimps, was enough for West and her company to be busted. She was found guilty of corrupting the morals of youth and sentenced to 10 days in prison. (She was released after two days for good behavior, a personality trait she spent her entire career studiously avoiding.)

In 1961 Lenny Bruce was arrested for obscenity in San Francisco for using the word *cocksucker*. That same year he was arrested in Los Angeles for using the word *schmuck*, which is Yiddish for penis. The arrests continued. In 1964 undercover cops attended Bruce's perfor-mance in New York and arrested him for obscenity. He was tried, found guilty, and sentenced to four months in prison. He appealed the verdict but died before the appeal was heard in court.

Oh brother, have times changed.

In 2011 a play titled *The Motherfucker with the Hat* opened on Broadway. The dialogue was a torrent of obscenities. The play was nominated for six Tony Awards, including Best Play. The only trace of concern about the language was the censoring of the title when it appeared in ads, in which it was called *The Motherf**ker with the Hat*.

Today, in comedy clubs throughout North America, jokes involving the most graphic sex acts, described in the most obscene language, are being told nonstop, every minute of the evening, every day of the week—including Christmas, Rosh Hashanah, and Kwanzaa.

"Anything goes" doesn't apply just to matters of sex; it also applies to social, political, and personal issues. Racism, for the first part of the 20th century, was a taboo subject in entertainment. The Sarah Silverman piece about her African American ex-boyfriend that appears in chapter 14 would, in the not-too-distant past, be unimaginable as stand-up comedy. As would Lisa Lampanelli's entire act. As the Queen of Mean, Lampanelli ladles out jokes that are racist, sexist, homophobic . . . let's cut to the chase: she offends everyone.

> Ladies, nothing wrong with your white husbands. But bang a black guy just once; it's worth the screwed-up credit . . . I bang a lot of black guys. That's my thing. It ain't by choice. I just haven't lost enough weight to get a white guy to fuck me. That's the problem . . . Any Middle Easterners here? 'Cause I don't smell anything. Are you here, you stinky bastards? They stink. When are those cabdrivers gonna learn, curry ain't no deodorant. "Strong enough for a man, made for a Hindu princess."
>
> I can tell from the way you are clapping, a big, dirty homosexual is right in the first row. I love the cornholers, oh yeah! You guys should see him. He's so gay he poops Skittles.

Disturbingly, this disregard for political correctness has spilled out of the arena of comedy, where it's offered up in fun, into the arena of politics—where power, not fun, is the goal. Here is a Lampanelli joke on Hispanics:

> (To a Hispanic audience member) I love that little spic. <u>I always wanted to bang you little bastards.</u> But my parents are those old-fashioned racist Italians. And you know the old saying, "Once you go Hispanic, woo! woo! <u>Mom and Dad start to panic.</u>" <u>Because you steal.</u>

And here is what Donald Trump said about Mexicans when he announced his candidacy for President:

> When Mexico sends its people, they're not sending their best. They're not sending you. They're not sending you. They're sending people that have lots of problems, and they're bringing those problems with us. They're bringing drugs. They're bringing crime. They're rapists. And some, I assume, are good people.

Many people believe that Mr. Trump's language is racist and poses a serious threat to the people he attacks and to our democracy. Certainly his language is a threat to Lisa Lampanelli's act. In terms of being edgy, what Lampanelli says about Hispanics pales next to what Trump is saying about them. It becomes more difficult to delight an audience with your naughty edginess when the president of the United States has said more outrageous things than you have.

This is the dilemma for edgy stand-ups: How can you entertain people by crossing the line of what's considered acceptable, when, apparently, there is no line to cross anymore? Louis C.K., whose jokes about hating his kids appear in chapter 9, told jokes on *Saturday Night Live* about how pedophilia must be really good if people risk going to jail for it. If pedophilia jokes can be performed on network television, have we reached the end of the line?

The answer, happily, is no. There will always be a future for edgy stand-up comedy. To understand why, we need to look to its past.

Decades ago, stand-ups lived in socially more conservative times. Unlike today's stand-ups, they ran a real risk to their careers and sometimes even to their physical safety when they took on controversial subjects and used offensive language. Their jokes took guts and conviction to perform. They saw injustices and prejudices that to them were intolerable and chose to confront them with their comedy.

Loretta Mary Aiken, the African American character comedian, was a pioneer of edgy stand-up comedy. She created the character Jackie "Moms" Mabley and performed stand-up as Moms for five decades, from the 1920s to the 1970s. She wore a housedress and a floppy knit hat, called her audience "my darlin' children," and appeared to be toothless.

She was far from toothless. She did material on female sexuality and racism when both subjects were taboo. Because of her gravelly voice, poor diction (from apparently lacking teeth), and heavy street accent, you had to listen hard to make out what Moms was saying. But she rewarded your effort with jokes that none of her contemporaries would dare to say.

Her jokes about her sexual needs and desires were performed at a time when many people were in denial about women having sexual needs and desires. It was particularly edgy to hear these ideas expressed by a toothless older black woman:

> Help me make it through the night. If you can make it for half an hour, you're all right with me!
> Don't kiss me! You might start something you can't finish.

Back then it was OK for a man to be seen with a younger woman, or to express desire for a younger woman. But it was taboo for an older woman to express desire for a young man. And so, here is Moms:

> You know Moms has been accused of liking young men. And I'm guilty. Ain't no old man do nothing for me. But bring me a message from a young man. That's all he can do.

Anytime you see me with my arms around any old man, I'm holdin' him for the police!

Here is Moms's advice to old men who still want to have sex:

Quit it if you can't do nothin' with it.

Unlike her comic creation, Loretta Mary Aiken was a lesbian. And unlike most of her contemporaries in and out of show business, she was open about it. As Moms, she was one of the first comedians to do gay material:

Two fellas walkin' down the street met another fella, say, "Hi queen." This other fella turned around and knocked one of 'em cold. Say, "Now when he comes to, tell 'em I'm no queen. And tell him my father and mother are still livin' . . . I'm a princess."

Because of a desire to cultivate a national audience, performers didn't (and still don't today) express animosity toward any region of our country. If you were a black entertainer in mid-20th-century America, arguably the last thing you'd want to do is express contempt for the South: until the late 1960s, black people were still being lynched there. For the sake of your career and physical well-being, you didn't joke about Southern racism. Unless you were Moms:

It's no crime to come from the South. It's a crime to go back there.
. . . I had to go back down home. I had to go back down there. The people down there are terrible. . . . Baby, its rough down there! It's rough down there, baby. I swear them people still think, you know, that we have to mind them. Do what they say, do. Some old Klans come by and say, "Mammy." I said, "No damn mammy! Mom! I don't know nothin' about no log cabin. I never seen no log cabin. Split-level in the suburbs, baby." Yeah, some old Klansman, talkin' about help

him pull off, you know, take his sheet (she pronounces *sheet*
so it sounds like *shit*) off. I said, "I don't take no sheet off
of nobody. Are you crazy?" Let him pull his own sheet off.
I left that place in a hurry. Yeah, the bloodhound run me
to the Greyhound and I split.

Moms Mabley used stand-up comedy to expose and ridicule racism wherever she encountered it. In a performance in Philadelphia
in the 1960s, she performed a routine that presaged by five decades
the Black Lives Matter movement. It was a time when court-ordered
school desegregation was causing nationwide racial unrest. The routine begins with her getting ticketed by a Philadelphia policeman for
just standing on the street in a white neighborhood. When she tells
the cop she wasn't doing anything, he tells her she's being arrested
for jaywalking. She gets nervous and takes out a piece of chewing
gum, and when she discards the wrapper she gets another ticket for
littering. Walking to the police station, they pass a bakery and Moms
gets the cop's permission to go in to buy a piece of cheesecake:

I'm crazy about cheesecake. I walked in there and everybody
stop eating and looked right at me. I said, "I don't want to go
to school with you, I just want a piece of cheesecake. That's
all I want."

On this subject, no region of the country and no group of people
were off-limits to Moms:

A colored fella walkin' down the street met another colored
fella. He was all beat up. He said, "Man what happened to you?
KKK? White People's Council? Who beat you up like that?"
He said, "No man. My own people done this to me. My own
people beat me up like this." "They beat you up for what?" "I
sold my house to a Puerto Rican."

Before Moms Mabley, comedians like Will Rogers and Bob Hope did smart and funny political jokes. But their tone was benign. They were written so that no one would be offended by them:

> I am not a member of any organized political party. I am a Democrat.
> ... The more you observe politics, the more you've got to admit that each party is worse than the other.

> —Will Rogers

> I always like to go to Washington, DC. It gives me a chance to visit my money. . . . It's so cold here in Washington that politicians have their hands in their own pockets.

> —Bob Hope

Moms Mabley's jokes dug far deeper into the body politic of the United States than any comedian who came before her. She employed stand-up comedy for new purposes—speaking openly about female sexuality and confronting this nation's gravest sin, racism. In this regard, Moms Mabley is the mother of edgy stand-up.

Lenny Bruce is the father.

Lenny Bruce achieved national fame as a stand-up in the late 1950s and 1960s. He accomplished this without the benefit of the usual star-maker—television. Television essentially blacklisted him. He was too controversial, too "sick," too "dirty" to appear on TV. Hugh Hefner booked Lenny on his television variety show, *Playboy After Dark*, and Steve Allen booked him on his talk show, *The Steve Allen Show*. That was about it. Lenny's fame and notoriety were based on his live performances in clubs and concert halls. Like Moms, he took stand-up comedy where it had never gone before. His jokes confronted the hypocrisies of the pillars of society, including politicians and religious leaders. In addition, he became renowned for comically exposing the illogic and sickness behind negative attitudes toward sex.

I skipped a day of my sophomore year at Mamaroneck High School to see Lenny Bruce perform in New York City. It was the most avant-garde performance I've ever experienced. It was disorienting. I experienced two things simultaneously that I'd never experienced simultaneously before: laughter and fear. I was laughing because his comedy was hilarious, and I was fearful because he was doing jokes about unspeakable things like masturbation and the Holy Cross. (Lenny later denied in court that he performed material that I had seen him perform. It saddened me to hear this. He was denying the performance of great stuff.)

Here was Lenny on the Catholic Church's relationship with the Jews. In 1965 the Vatican issued a document stating that Christ's death could no longer be attributed to all of the Jewish people. The belief that Jews were and still are responsible for the act of deicide fueled European anti-Semitism and laid the groundwork for the Nazi holocaust. Lenny believed that by absolving Jews of this crime, the Church was further establishing Jewish guilt. He said it this way:

> There's been a lot of controversy lately on whether or not the Jews killed Christ. I'd like to settle this matter once and for all. We killed him; if he comes back, we'll kill him again.

It took guts and conviction for a black woman to create comedy about racism. It took guts and conviction for a Jewish man to create comedy about Christian anti-Semitism.

In the 1960s Lenny became a target of police arrests for obscenity. The stress of these constant arrests, combined with his drug addiction, led to the deterioration of his comedy and his career, and ultimately to his early death from an overdose of morphine in 1966.

Christians believe that Christ died for our sins. Comedians should be aware that Lenny died so we can sin.

Sam Kinison picked up the mantle from Lenny Bruce. From the mid-1980s to his death at age 38 in 1992, Kinison went after the big subjects—religion, politics, sexuality. Before he began his comedy career, Kinison was a Pentecostal preacher. He brought the hellfire-and-brimstone delivery that he used as a preacher to his stand-up persona. Kinison was at his edgiest and funniest when his subject was Christianity. He produced outrageously funny stand-up by applying simple logic to the Christian Bible. Here he is on perhaps the most sacred of Christian beliefs, the Resurrection:

Jesus had a tough life. I read about that guy. Jesus is the only guy that ever came back from the dead that didn't scare the FUCK out of everybody! He's the only guy that ever crawled out of a grave where people didn't go, "Oh—OOOHHHH!!! I JUST SAW SOME FUCKER CRAWL OUT OF HIS GRAVE! I DON'T BELIEVE I'M SEEIN' THIS SHIT! DID YOU SEE THAT? THIS GUY JUST CRAWLED OUT OF HIS BOX THROUGH THE EARTH!" People are losing it, going "Oh— OOOHHHH!!! THE DEAD LIVE! THE DEAD LIVE!!" (Trudging around like a zombie, making guttural noises.) "GET A STAKE—PUT A STAKE IN HIS ASS! CUT OFF HIS HEAD! KILL HIM AGAIN!!!" Jesus comes back—HE doesn't get any pressure, no static. Nobody's upset. He climbs out, he's walkin' around—nobody's upset. They can eat with him and everything. (Two men confiding in each other) "Hey—isn't that guy dead?" "Yeah, he is, man, but he won't accept it." (As Jesus, eyes rolled back in head as he eats) "Pass the butter . . . (buttering his bread) What are they starin' at???"

Moms Mabley, Lenny Bruce, and Sam Kinison are among the stand-ups who light the way to edgy comedy's perennial future. What they had in common was that they went after the most dangerous taboo subjects of their times. And they did it not only because it was a comically edgy thing to do, they did it because they had genuine convictions about righting wrongs and about exposing absurdity, hypocrisy, and mendacity among the powerful and exalted. What gives the best edgy comedy its bite is that behind the shockingly outrageous jokes are deeply held convictions.

Today the taboos may be harder to find, but they're still here and always will be. Look hard enough and you'll see the devil is still citing Scripture. Look hard enough and you'll see what the great comic playwright George Bernard Shaw saw in his own time and place: Our problem is not that we fail to live up to our ideals. Our problem is that too often we do live up to them, and too many of them are corrupt and self-serving.

The really great edgy stand-ups shock audiences as a means of jolting them into confronting inconvenient truths about themselves and their ways of living. One of the greatest comedy writers of all time, the French playwright Molière, instructs us:

The duty of comedy is to correct men by entertaining them.

I'll drink to that, mon ami.

17

SPECIALTIES

IN ADDITION TO CLASSIC STAND-UP in which the comedian talks to the audience, there are specialty forms of stand-up. There are comedians who use props; there are comedians who do impressions of famous people; there are comedians who use magic in their acts; and there are comedians who incorporate music into their acts. There are also comedy teams and ventriloquists.

Like all the forms of stand-up comedy, specialties may be used along with other forms, or they can become the entire act. For instance, there are stand-ups who might do celebrity impressions in just a few of their jokes, and then there are impressionists like Rich Little whose entire act is performing impressions. There are stand-ups who might play a song or two, and there are comedians like the great Victor Borge, whose entire act was performed at the piano.

In incorporating these or any other elements into your stand-up, be aware that performing your specialty may present special challenges. If you use props, you have to schlep them to the club and figure out where to put them onstage so you can get to them and get rid of them easily. Most comedy clubs don't have pianos, so if your act requires one, you may need to bring your own electronic keyboard and maybe your own amp to the club. Think out the special requirements of your act and make sure either that the club has what you need, or that you can provide it yourself and make it work at the club.

To successfully perform a specialty, you have to get really good at it. You have to nail your impression, your song, your magic trick. You don't get a pass because you're performing these feats as part of your comedy. Performing the specialties well is a requirement of doing them at all.

Of course, you can also get laughs by appearing not to do the specialty well. Jack Benny sometimes played a violin in his act. He made a big deal about how great he was at it, and then played awfully. As he screeched out notes that were so off-key you could barely make out what tune he was playing, his face radiated ecstasy. If you muted the sound, he looked like a virtuoso violinist swooning at the heavenly sounds he was creating. Turn the volume up and there was Jack, as oblivious to how awful his musicianship was as he was oblivious to his miserliness. Playing that badly took skill, and Jack Benny had it. He was a professional violinist before he became a comedian.

Doing the specialty well, however, is not enough to make it a stand-up piece. If you sing in your act, you not only have to sing well, you have to sing funny. Taking a well-known song and replacing its lyrics with your own comic lyrics is a staple of stand-up comedy. "Weird Al" Yankovic has made a career doing this. Here, for example, is an excerpt from his rewrite of the pop hit "Girls Just Want to Have Fun." He calls it "Girls Just Want to Have Lunch":

> *I know how to keep a woman satisfied*
> *When I whip out my Diner's Card their eyes get so wide*
> *They're always in the mood for something to munch*
> *Oh, girls, they wanna have lunch . . .*

This form can be incredibly effective in delivering frequent laughs. In a well-written comedy song, each rhyming word can be a laugh. Comically rhymed lyrics can create as many as six to eight laughs per minute. That's an excellent laughs-per-minute ratio.

The great comedian Bert Lahr made the very act of singing funny. Watch him sing "If I Were King of the Forest" in *The Wizard of Oz*. The lyrics are clever, but not funny. What's funny is the way he sings. A vibrato in singing is a rapid and very slight variation in pitch that makes the tone sound richer. His vibrato spans entire notes and goes on hilariously too long.

If you do impressions in your stand-up, it's not enough to master the speech and physicality of the celebrity you're impersonating. You need to create comedy with your impression. This can be done by exaggerating one of the celebrity's vocal or physical traits; Jimmy Stewart's stammer, for instance, made him a favorite among impressionists. Another way to create comedy with an impression is to put the celebrity into a situation for which he's hilariously mismatched. At a roast for the master insult comedian Don Rickles, Rich Little did an impression of Rickles as president of the United States greeting foreign leaders to the White House for a peace conference. "President" Rickles, of course, insulted each one of them:

King Faisal of Saudi Arabia. <u>So, so, so, so</u> glad you could come. <u>Hope you can find a parking place for your camel. Anyway,</u> <u>may I say something your highness? And I say this from the</u> <u>bottom of my heart. You gotta be the ugliest king I've ever</u> <u>seen in my life.</u>

If you want to perform stand-up with a partner, it's not enough for each of you to have funny jokes. You have to have a comic relationship and a clear reason why you're onstage together. The Smothers Brothers are brothers. George Burns and Gracie Allen were husband and wife. Dean Martin and Jerry Lewis were best friends, as were Dan Rowan and Dick Martin. In addition to a reason for your relationship, there has to be comedy in the relationship itself. In between performing folk songs, the Smothers Brothers engaged in fierce sibling rivalry that usually led to Tommy Smothers pouting, "Mom always liked you best," his signature line.

Gracie Allen used the form of the comic flaw to create a lovable ditz. Her husband, George, was her straight man, who set up her laugh lines and helped the audience make sense of she was saying.

GRACIE ALLEN: Oh my, the department stores were crowded today! I was at the exchange desk and the girl was out to lunch so we all had to wait in line. And I was seven.

GEORGE BURNS: Well, that's your lucky number.

ALLEN: I asked the lady in front of me what she was exchanging, and she said, um, "Well, I have to return these shoes for my children. They're too tight." And I said, "Shame on you <u>for allowing your children to drink.</u>"

BURNS: Well that was telling her.

ALLEN: Mmhmm. Then the line <u>moved up and I was six.</u>

BURNS: Oh the, the girl came back from lunch?

ALLEN: No. The woman in front of me <u>went to the back of the line.</u>

BURNS: Back of the line, I should have known.

ALLEN: Oh, and then the man ahead of me, uh, he looked so peculiar. He had a lot of hair on the side of his head, but none on top. So I said to him, I said, "My, you must have grown fast when you were a boy. <u>You grew right up through your hair!</u>"

BURNS: Uhh, that was a nice way to break the ice!

If you want to create stand-up comedy by doing magic tricks, your performance of the tricks and/or the tricks themselves need to be funny. Steve Martin, in a performance on *The Smothers Brothers Comedy Hour*, performed the well-known zombie floating ball trick. In the standard performance of the trick, the magician shows the audience a ball. He then places the ball on a small pedestal on the table. He covers the ball with a cloth. The magician then recites magic words and the ball, whose outline is clearly visible under the cloth, magically rises. The magician recites more magic words and the magic ball appears again, and seems to be balanced on the top of the cloth. The magician once again covers the ball with the cloth. It continues its flight until the magician commands the ball to return to the pedestal, which it does.

When Martin performed the trick and commanded the ball to return to the pedestal, it didn't. It took on a life of its own. It refused to pay any attention to Martin and proceeded to fly offstage with Martin helplessly in tow. As performed by Steve Martin, the trick succeeded as comedy and as magic.

Ventriloquism requires the mastery of many crafts. A ventriloquist must be able to do a variety of voices and accents. He must be able to throw his voice so it appears to be coming, not from him, but from a dummy. He needs to acquire the skill of speaking without moving his lips. He needs to work with a dummy maker to create characters whose personalities are clearly visible on their faces. Jeff Dunham is one of the leading ventriloquists of our time. His main dummy, Walter, doesn't even need to talk for us to know he's a disapproving sourpuss: his downturned mouth is a permanent frown, his eyes are a mistrustful squint, and his arms are folded in a gesture of unrelenting disapproval. The ventriloquist must also master how to manipulate the dummy so that it appears to be alive. Bringing these skills together, the ventriloquist creates vivid characters who become his onstage comedy partners.

Then he must write comedy that highlights the dummies' personas. Walter's jokes key off his negativity and disapproval. The comedy written for Achmed the Dead Terrorist, also a Dunham character, keys off his unsuccessful attempts to terrorize people:

DUNHAM: Good evening, Achmed.
ACHMED: Good evening, infidel!
DUNHAM: So you're a terrorist?
ACHMED: Yes. I am a terrorist.
DUNHAM: What kind of terrorist?
ACHMED: A terrifying (looks back and forth with only his eyes as if to scare everyone) terrorist. Are you scared?
DUNHAM: Not really, no.

ACHMED: AAWRR!... And now?!

DUNHAM: Not really, no.

ACHMED: AAHH ARRRRR!!... How about now?

DUNHAM: No.

ACHMED: Goddammit.... Oh! Oh. I mean, uh, Allah dammit! (To audience) Silence!... I kill you!

(Achmed gives the audience a threatening look. The audience laughs and claps.)

Terry Fator is another master ventriloquist and impersonator. His dummy Maynard Thompkins claims to be the greatest Elvis impersonator in the world. He wears an Elvis-style glittery Las Vegas cape, sports an Elvis haircut, and has Elvis sideburns. The comedy written for Maynard keys off his inability to sing an Elvis song. He says that he gets so nervous when he's in front of people that he can't sing—out loud, that is. He assures us that when he sings in his head he's a dead ringer for Elvis. Nerves aren't the only reason he can't sing Elvis songs. He doesn't know any. The comedy heats up as Fator becomes increasingly irritated with Maynard. Finally, Maynard ends the act by convincingly singing, à la Elvis, a medley of the most famous Elvis songs. When Fator asks him why he said he didn't know any Elvis songs, Maynard replies that he didn't know those songs were Elvis's. Fator successfully combines all the skills of a ventriloquist, an impersonator, a singer, and a stand-up.

If, in addition to your talent for stand-up, you have other gifts as a performer, integrating those gifts into your act can be satisfying for you and delightful for your audience. Remember, the key is to get good at your specialty—and make it funny.

18

AD-LIBBING

EACH OF THE PERFORMING ARTS can seem impossible to do. When plays have talk-backs—events where the audience is invited to stay after the play's conclusion to talk to the actors—the one question that is always asked is, "How can you memorize all of those lines?" Opera singers create sounds that are so powerful, so rich, so wide-ranging that their ability to sing seems superhuman. Dancers appear to have the power to switch off gravity. The impossible thing that stand-ups appear able to do is to be spontaneously funny night after night. It's like magic.

In fact, it is like magic. Because it's a trick. The trick is to learn how to deliver written material in a way that seems so spontaneous, the audience thinks you're making it up on the spot. When I first started studying stand-up comedy, I would spend an evening following one stand-up from club to club to see how his act would differ. What I discovered was, it didn't. I remember a stand-up who began his evening at the original Improv in New York. In the middle of his act, he momentarily lost his train of thought and said, "Wait a minute. There was something else I wanted to talk to you guys about. Oh, got it." And then he'd proceed to his next joke. He played three clubs that night and at each club, in exactly the same place in his set, he did his "Wait a minute" routine. And so he spun the illusion that he was just an incredibly funny guy who was talking to us off the top of his head about things he'd just thought of a moment ago. In fact, he was performing his written set word for word. I named this technique a *thought moment*. This is when a stand-up creates the illusion of spontaneity by pretending to need a moment to regain his train of thought.

When a stand-up has a paid gig at a major club, he performs his written act. He may ad-lib just a little, if he's good at it. It may appear that he's riffing the entire time he's up there. But in fact he's performing his tried-and-true material, the stuff that consistently gets big laughs. When a club pays you to perform, and an audience pays to see you perform, you can't take the risk of ad-libbing your entire set. Material that has never been performed before is bound to be hit and miss. That's the case for everyone, including comedy's most famous performers and writers.

Where you can see big-name stand-ups riffing is at showcase clubs. The regular performers at these clubs are good local stand-ups, not famous headliners. When famous headliners appear at showcase clubs, they are unannounced. The fact that no one has paid to see them gives them the license to riff and try new material. They can't do this at headliner clubs where they're paid big money to reliably deliver a great show. The venues for new stand-ups to try out new material are stand-up comedy classes and open mics.

There's an exception to this rule about not ad-libbing at paid gigs. His name is Jonathan Winters. His ability to ad-lib was beyond what is humanly possible. He may not have been from here, and by "here" I mean Earth. Go to YouTube and search "Jonathan Winters The Stick." You'll see him improvise a four-minute set on national television. It is indescribably funny (which means I can't do it justice by describing it), so go now and watch it. I'll wait for you. Go.

Jonathan Winters is the only stand-up I know of who achieved and sustained stardom by ad-libbing. But the odds are that when you make your national television debut, you won't be standing backstage right before showtime wondering what you're going to say.

Ad-libbing is not a form of stand-up comedy that is performed at clubs. It is, however, the genesis of all comedy. You spontaneously think and say funny things, and that's an important part of creating the first draft of your stand-up material. This brings us to the next section of the book.

Part III

THE HANDBOOK FOR CREATING STAND-UP COMEDY MATERIAL

19

PREPARING FOR YOUR FIRST DRAFT

Now that you have a grasp of the forms your stand-up comedy material can take, and you've seen how other stand-ups have employed these forms to create their material, it's time for you to start writing your own material. In these next three chapters I'm going to lay out a writing process for you. It's designed to help you create comedy material that is:

- Original
- Written in your distinctive comic voice
- Tightly written—thus enabling you to deliver lots of laughs to your audience

We're going to take this step by step. Here is step one:

Believe You Are a Comedy Writer

Here's a question I get asked a lot: "I make my friends laugh, but that doesn't mean I can write stand-up comedy, right?" Here's the answer: Remember, when you make your friends laugh, you are writing stand-up comedy with your mouth. People write stand-up comedy with their pens, pencils, keyboards, and their mouths. These are all equally good ways of writing. The only difference with writing with your mouth is that it requires one additional step. You or someone else has to write down what you say. So whether or not you have ever put pen to paper, or fingers to a keyboard—if you have made people laugh, you are a comedy writer.

Sometimes people who haven't written comedy before think of comedy writers as wizards, possessed of magical powers inaccessible to mere mortals. This is not true. For a person who knows how to make people laugh, comedy writing is work—nothing more, nothing less. And the harder you work at it, the better you get. I'm believer in this maxim: talent is work, and brilliance is obsession with work. I'm lingering on this point to make sure you do the following: think of "comedy writer" as a hat, and put it on your head and keep it there.

Capture Your Sense of Humor

Your next step as a comedy writer is to capture your sense of humor. In the past, before you read this paragraph, you'd say something funny to friends or family, they'd laugh, and that was that. Not anymore. Funny is too valuable to be treated that way.

Let me give you an example of just how valuable it can be. I once spoke with an investor in big-budget Hollywood comedies. I asked him if he had some system that helped him choose which movies to invest in. He said he did: He would read the script and determine, as best he could, how many "A" laughs it contained. (An "A" laugh, sometimes called a *house laugh*, means everyone in the house is laughing loudly.) According to his research, every "A" laugh in a Hollywood movie is worth $7 million at the box office. He would count the "A" laughs and multiply them by 7 million. If that figure was significantly higher than the film's budget, he was interested. Then he would look at other factors, such as the director and the cast, and make his decision. But for him, star directors and actors only count when there are enough big laughs in the script.

"A" laughs are valuable commodities. When you get good at writing and performing material that consistently delivers them, people will start paying you. So get good at capturing what you *think*, *say*, *hear*, and *see* that is funny. Write these things down or voice-record them. In an interview in the *Paris Review*, Woody Allen described how he gets started on a new project:

> I'll think of an idea walking down the street, and I'll mark it down immediately.

Good advice. Follow it.

Don't Steal

In my list of funny things to write down, I include funny things that you hear. By this I mean funny things you hear from family and friends, on the street, at work, at parties—funny things you hear in real life. NOT funny things that other stand-ups say in their acts; or funny things that you read; or funny things you hear in movies, television, and the theater; or funny things you see on the Internet. Do not steal jokes. Let me explain what I mean by this.

Stealing a joke means copying word for word or paraphrasing another stand-up's or comedy writer's material. If you write jokes about *subjects* that other comedians talk or write about, that's not stealing. No one can own a subject. But a person does own his or her *words* about a subject. When you steal a joke you're committing an act of plagiarism and harming the livelihood and/or legacy of a fellow comedian. You may also find yourself sued for copyright infringement.

Here's another reason you shouldn't steal jokes: The Internet has made it much easier to call out comedy plagiarists. And when that happens, careers are ruined.

In an earlier era, a big-name comedian could steal jokes from lesser-known comedians and perform them on television or in Vegas with impunity. There was no way short of an expensive and risky lawsuit for an unknown stand-up to prove that he told his joke before the star comedian did. Milton Berle, the most famous comedian on television in its earliest days, was a notorious joke thief—his nickname among his fellow comedians was "the Thief of Bad Gag." He didn't even deny it; he once joked to Larry King, "I don't steal people's jokes. I just find them before they're lost." His open thievery never damaged his career. In fact, so many people wanted to see his show that he's credited with selling millions of television sets and establishing television as the most popular form of mass entertainment of its time. He became known as Mr. Television.

But if Berle were stealing jokes and using them on television today, in the era of the Internet, he'd be toast. A salient example of how the Internet has made it easier for stand-ups to protect their material is the case of Carlos Mencia. Mencia had his own comedy show on Comedy Central in the mid-2000s. The show made him one of stand-up comedy's biggest and most powerful stars. But that didn't stop him from being outed as a flagrant joke thief by a then much lesser-known stand-up named Joe Rogan. In 2007, Rogan posted a video online (it's still available on YouTube: "Joe Rogan VS Carlos Mencia") that proved Mencia stole jokes from Rogan and a variety of other stand-ups. The video led to Mencia's show being canceled by Comedy Central and dealt a fatal blow to his career as both a television and comedy club superstar.

So, don't steal. The Internet can catch you and nail you for it.

There is a third reason not to steal material: if the stolen jokes are any good, they're infused with the persona of the stand-up who created them. You want your jokes to be infused with your persona, to communicate who you are to your audiences. I recall a show at the original Improv where, to my utter shock, a young, preppy comedian started doing, word for word, material from Woody Allen's famous comedy piece "Hasidic Tales." Written in a style that parodies 19th-century Eastern European Yiddish authors, the story is about a Middle-European Jew searching for the answer to the question "Why can't we Jews eat pork?" And this poster boy for Connecticut WASPdom was attempting to pass it off as his own. I couldn't stand it. I started booing. Loudly. I started yelling, "That's Woody Allen's material." No one stopped me so I kept going until I drove him off the stage. I'd never done that before; never done it since. I was a young hothead then. I like to think I've matured. Now, I'm an old hothead. Don't steal, OK?

Stand-Up Comedy Subjects

Now that you're about to embark on writing original stand-up comedy material, it would be helpful, I believe, to provide you with the complete list of stand-up comedy subjects, so you can see the full range of things you can talk about in your stand-up. Here's the list:

- **Subject 1:** How you feel about your life. (Your life in the past, your life now, and what you think your life will be in the future)
- **Subject 2:** How you feel about everything else that matters to you. (Politics, celebrities, pop culture, food, fashions, technology, etc.)

End of list. The reason I said earlier in this chapter that it's inevitable you will talk about subjects that other stand-ups talk about too is that there are, essentially, only two subjects.

It's illuminating to compare this list of stand-up comedy subjects to another art form's list of subjects, painting. You can paint:

- **Subject 1:** How you see what is outdoors
- **Subject 2:** How you see what is indoors
- **Subject 3:** How you see what you are experiencing inside yourself

End of list. The shortness of both of these lists raises a question: How can you be original when there are so few subjects? The answer is that in stand-up, as in all art forms, the real subject is *you*.

Let's go back to painting for a moment. In the permanent collection of the Museum of Modern Art in New York is the famous Van

Gogh painting *Starry Night*. In the rare instances when this painting is lent out to other cities' museums, thousands of people line up to see it. Why? Are they waiting in line and prepared to pay an entrance fee to see a starry night? If that were the case, they could just wait until there was a real starry night and look up. No line, no fee. It's not the subject of starry nights that draws art lovers from around the world to gaze at Van Gogh's painting, it's the experience of seeing a starry night through his eyes and sensibility. No one has experienced a starry night and rendered it in a painting the way he did. Through his eyes it is a celestial night ablaze, and thrilling to look at.

This same dynamic is at play in stand-up comedy material. What ultimately gives your writing originality and freshness is not your subject, but your way with the subject—how you think and feel about it.

That being said, there's no denying that everybody has unique life experiences, and certainly these experiences are rich resources for stand-up material. Olga Namer is a student of mine who comes from a devoutly Orthodox Jewish family and community, a unique life experience that has given rise to excellent material like this:

(Olga chants a prayer in Hebrew.)

That is a prayer I said for twenty-four years of my life, until I found out it said, "Bless the God creator of the universe, thank you for not making me a woman." I was like, "Rabbi! What the fuck?!" He's like, "No, that's the man's prayer; the woman's prayer is on the next page: 'Bless the God creator of the universe, thank you for not making me a slave.'" I was like, "Tell that to my ex-husband, Yehuda."

. . . I moved to the West Village, and I started hanging out with my old boyfriend Bob. He's not an ex, he's just old. He's also a gentile. He was like forbidden fruit, rotten and nearly expired. When I told my parents about Bob they were like, "If you continue dating him, we're gonna disown you." And immediately I was like, "Oh my God, what? . . . We have money?" They were like, "No," so I was like, "So what are you gonna disown me from?" They were like, **"You're not gonna be on the Verizon family plan anymore!"**

It isn't Olga's subjects, however, that ultimately account for the originality of her material. Olga is rebelling against her family and her religion. Looked upon in this light, these are not original subjects. Lots of comedians deal with them. What is original is her way with these subjects, not the subjects themselves.

To clarify this point, let's look at arguably one of the least original of subjects: food. Can you create fresh, original stand-up comedy material about such a common subject? If you realize that the real subject is your sensibility about food, yes. In fact, my former student Jim Gaffigan has achieved a hugely successful comedy career around this one subject. Over the course of many years, Jim's relationship with food has been an endless source of material for his stand-up, his two books *Dad Is Fat* and *Food: A Love Story*, and his television series, *The Jim Gaffigan Show*. Here is Jim on his feelings about bacon:

> What makes breakfast in bed so special, is that you're lying down and eating bacon, the most beautiful thing on Earth. Bacon's the best. Even the frying of bacon sounds like applause. It's like: **"HAAAAAAAA. (High-pitched voice) Yaaayy! Bacon!!"** You wanna know how good bacon is? To improve other food, they wrap it in bacon. If it weren't for bacon, we wouldn't even know what a water chestnut is. **"Thank you, bacon. Sincerely, Water Chestnut the Third."**
> . . . Whenever you're at a brunch buffet and you see that big metal tray filled with the four thousand pieces of bacon . . . don't you almost expect a rainbow to be coming out of it? **"I found it, I found the source of all bacon!"** That bacon tray is always at the end of the buffet; you regret all the stuff on your plate. **"What am I doing with all this worthless fruit? I should have waited! If I had known you were here I would have waited!"**

To start with, Jim is slightly chubby. We know from this that when he talks about food, it's a subject that occupies a place of real significance in his life. It's not just that Jim has a voracious appetite; Jim adores food. Food doesn't mean the world to Jim. Food *is* the world to Jim. Not only is he completely unapologetic about that, but he gets grouchy with people who don't get it. For Jim, eating delicious, fatty, greasy, unhealthy food is the reason to live. All of that—his chubbiness, his adoration of unhealthy food, his grouchiness toward people who don't get his food-centric way of life—is what powers his comedy. His subject isn't food. His subject is the meaning of life, which, according to Jim, is food.

Now that you consider yourself (1) a comedy writer; (2) not just any comedy writer, but one who knows to immediately write down your funny ideas; and (3) a comedy writer who understands that the real subject of your stand-up comedy is yourself—your feelings and opinions on the subjects you're talking about—it's time to start the first draft!

20

THE FIRST DRAFT

THERE IS A CHALLENGING DISCIPLINE involved in creating a successful first draft, and it comes into play right at the outset: **Do not throw anything out.** Here is a rookie mistake: You say something funny, people laugh, you write it down. Three days later you look at the scrap of paper, read the words you spoke three days ago, and think, *This isn't funny. What was I thinking?* So you throw it out.

Big mistake. In writing comedy, nothing gets *thrown* out until it's *tried* out. If you think something is funny even for a nanosecond, write it down and hold on to it: the odds are that something funny is there. There is no editing, no second-guessing, in writing a first draft. Think of yourself as a psychic, a medium whose job is simply to record the words that you hear in the comedy ether. Once you hear them, write them down and don't look back. The only way to know for sure if something is funny is to try it out in front of people. An audience will tell you what to edit out. That's their job, not yours. At this initial stage, your job is to come up with funny ideas for material. The first draft is the time to generate and write down as much material as comes to your mind. It is not a time to eliminate. It is a time to add. Turn on the faucet of your sense of humor and let it run, let it run, let it run. Rant, rave, go on and on, and **do not get in your own way.**

Sometimes comedians I work with tell me they have writer's block. They can't come up with new material. The well has run dry. Actually it hasn't. Let me explain.

Sense of humor is an accurate description of how funny things come to you. It is one of your senses. You have a sense of sight, smell, taste, touch, hearing—and humor. Seeing the future is not your sixth sense. Seeing what's funny is. Unless you were born with a disability, or sustained a serious injury, or contracted a serious disease, all of your senses are operative, including your sense of humor.

Writer's block, therefore, is not caused by your sense of humor disappearing; it's caused by you *rejecting* your sense of humor. The problem isn't that you've stopped coming up with funny ideas but that you're snuffing them out as soon as you have them. You're not letting them see the light of day. You're not doing what you need to do to discover if something is funny or not: write it down and try it out. The cure to writer's block is to stop editing yourself. Write down your funny ideas and add to them.

What follows are some specific things *not* to be concerned about when you're writing your first draft.

Don't worry if you're going too long before getting to a laugh. Sometimes what we initially think is a setup to a joke turns out to be the punchline, and you don't want to mistakenly cut it because you think you don't need it. As an example, let's revisit the opening of Kate Redway's piece about the Bible. Here's the first draft of her opening joke on that subject:

> I don't go to church anymore. All they read is the Bible. And I already read that. Can't they read something else, for Chris-sake?!

When Kate tried this joke out in our workshop and later at the Gotham Comedy Club, we learned from the audience response that the line "And I already read that" is not a setup line, but the punchline. The audience taught us that. Trying out the material will enable you to locate where the laughs are. Once you have a good sense of this, you'll be in position to make cuts without inadvertently cutting laugh lines.

Don't worry about making transitions from one funny idea to another in your first draft. You don't know yet what the order of your jokes will be. Develop each funny idea as a stand-alone piece of material. Once the first draft is developed into tightly written jokes, you will determine how to order the material and how to get it to flow. That doesn't happen in a first draft, so don't concern yourself with it.

Don't worry about wandering off your subject. It's *good* to wander. You may start with one idea and then wander into something else, and that something else can turn out to be comedy gold.

A good example of this is an experience I once had writing material about *The Sopranos* for Rock Albers, the two-time MAC Award–winning stand-up and my former student. The series was in its second or third season and had established itself as a gigantic hit. With my voice recorder on, I was riffing about the New Jersey mob and found myself talking about the title sequence of each Sopranos episode, which is a montage of shots showing Tony Soprano, the mob boss, driving home from New York City to his mansion in New Jersey.

The first sequence of shots shows Tony driving through the Lincoln Tunnel. For readers who are not from the New York–New Jersey area, let me explain that people who commute through this tunnel hate it. The rush-hour traffic jams through the Lincoln Tunnel are nightmares, so awful that they suppress the real estate value of homes in New Jersey. When I told friends that we were moving from our New York City apartment to a house in New Jersey, the usual response wasn't "Oh, you're getting a house in New Jersey!" It was "Oh God, that tunnel!!" So here's what I said about the Sopranos:

I don't understand what the big mystery is about why Tony Soprano is so violent. He keeps going to see a psychiatrist when the reason is so obvious: in front of every single episode, week after week, year after year, <u>they make the man drive through the Lincoln Tunnel! Of course he wants to kill people!</u>

Once I got started on the subject of the tunnel, I kept going:

> This is what we named after Lincoln? <u>Didn't this man suffer</u>
> <u>enough? We should name it the John Wilkes Booth Tunnel or</u>
> <u>the Mariah Carey Tunnel.</u>

The jokes that ended up in Rock's act were the jokes about the tunnel. The only Sopranos joke was the one about Tony's rage about the tunnel. We didn't plan it that way; it just happened. We knew not to get in the way, not to stop the riff because it was going off the subject. As a result, we got several new terrific jokes.

Don't worry whether it's funny or not. What we're looking for in a first draft are strong comic ideas—funny ideas. You may have a strong comic idea but not quite the right wording for it. If the comic idea is strong, you'll find the precise wording that gets the laughs in the process of rewriting and performing the material.

Don't worry about whether your idea is original. Unless you're actually stealing another stand-up's joke, writing it down word for word or consciously paraphrasing it, you're not stealing anything. Remember, nobody owns a subject.

Don't worry about anything. Just write it down. The time will come to ruthlessly cut, tighten, and rewrite. The first draft is not the time.

If you're comfortable on the computer, use it. If you prefer writing things down on paper, fine. If you like to "write" with your mouth and record what you say, terrific. If you feel that writing down a joke or recording it destroys its spontaneity, then hear this: I've worked with successful stand-ups who never write down their jokes. They're a small minority, but they exist. They all have one thing in common: photographic memories. They retain word for word what they've said. They rewrite and refine their jokes in their heads, not on paper. Once they've found the exact wording that makes their jokes work, they stick to it word for word. If you don't have a photographic memory, this is not the way for you to work. Write things down or voice-record them.

Part of the craft and art of performing stand-up comedy is creating the illusion that you're being spontaneous onstage. There's a word for creating this illusion: acting. Just as a skilled scriptwriter finds the best way to phrase a line, the gifted stand-up comedy writer finds the best way to word a joke. When that happens—and you know it's happened from the big laughs you consistently get from audiences—there is no longer room for improvements. Rephrasing it will only hurt it, and perhaps kill the laugh. At that point, the joke is set and performed word for word. Through his ability as an actor, the stand-up creates the illusion that the words he has performed time and again are popping out of his mouth for the first time.

It's time to get started. I give my workshop students two assignments to get them going. These prompts reliably generate "A" jokes. Here's the first one:

Write about people, places, and things that annoy the hell out of you.

People to whom you are closest sometimes annoy you the most—your significant other, family, and friends. People at work or at school can annoy you. People you deal with occasionally or casually do annoying things—the bus driver, your dry cleaner, your landlord, your doctors. Strangers do annoying things—people you're in line with, people at the laundromat, clerks at the DMV, at the Apple Store, the drugstore. Celebrities from the world of entertainment, politics, and sports can annoy you. And, of course, *you* do things that annoy you.

Places can annoy you: bus and train stations, airports, your hometown, your school, place of business, place of worship, prisons, military bases, supermarkets, delis, restaurants, malls, department stores, health clubs, and so on.

Things can annoy you: diets, shopping, working, studying, dating, partying, clubbing, playing and watching sports, watching TV, videos, politics, sex, music, vacations, holidays, weddings, anniversaries, birthdays, funerals, reunions, wakes, websites, magazines, books, movies, computers, phones, etc.

Feel free to use any of these subjects and also feel free to add to the lists.

The second assignment is:

Write about anything you want.

In carrying out these assignments, if you want to write things down word for word the way you would say it onstage, fine. If you want to create your first draft with your mouth, and work off of notes, or just riff, fine. But be sure to voice-record yourself while you're riffing. When you're done, play back your recording and write down what you said, word for word, on paper. **And don't throw anything out!**

To help you get started, I'm going to provide you with a sample first draft written by Laura Bassi. In the stand-up excerpts that appear in earlier chapters, the laugh lines have been underlined based on where club audiences actually laughed. See if you can guess where the laughs are in this untested first draft, and underline them. Let's see how your guesses match up to where the club audiences actually laughed. Getting good at sensing this is important to developing your comedy-writing skills.

Here is Laura's first draft of a piece about what we teach little kids:

Everyone tries to teach their kids animal sounds because it's cute, but half the sounds aren't even what the animals say . . . What does the cow say? Moo? Umm, like, why is that a thing we teach kids? No animal sounds like that. You don't go to a zoo and hear the pigs going oink oink . . . you hear them and they're, like (makes real pig sound), and no one wants their children walking around doing that noise. We should really approach it from a different angle, like, "What do pigs think?" And the answer is, "Please don't slaughter me into tiny pieces, then reprocess me into that lunch-meat ham you love on your deli sandwiches." This doesn't help them with their life. Let's help them. Sometimes men are pigs. So what do pigs say? "Dang, girl, you look good. Come over here." Why not use this format to teach them other things so they know what to do with their lives: What does the twenty-seven-year-old with no career who is taking care of you right now say? "HELP!!"

21

TRYING OUT
YOUR FIRST DRAFT

"Where should I try out my first draft?" That is a crucially important question.

Established stand-ups try out new material at small comedy clubs. Typically, the new material is interspersed with tried-and-true material—material that has proven to reliably deliver up laughs. This way, if the new jokes don't do well, there are still plenty of solid jokes in the set to entertain the audience. There is no better way to evaluate new material than performing it in front of a paying audience. Paying audiences have only one purpose for attending a show: they want to be entertained. This inclines them to pay attention to the performers rather than chattering among themselves. It makes them eager to laugh at the funny stuff. Just as important, they feel no obligation to laugh at the unfunny stuff. They are, without question, the ultimate editor in chief of stand-up comedy material.

Stand-ups who are in the early stages of their comedy careers don't have this option. But they have others. If you're reading this book in conjunction with taking a class or a workshop in stand-up up comedy, you'll try out your first draft in front of your teacher and classmates. You'll get feedback and suggestions from them on what to keep as is, what has potential but needs rewriting, and what material to toss.

It's essential that you voice-record yourself while you're performing in class. Suggestions from teachers and peers can be useful. But the most reliable feedback you can get is laughter. Where they laugh will point you to where the jokes are. When you're in a class or workshop, any laugh, even if it's just a titter from one person, counts as a laugh. Later, when you perform the material in a club in front of a paying audience, your standards for what constitutes a laugh will be far more stringent. But when you're in class, little laughs count.

Classes and workshops offer the opportunity to be mentored by a teacher. A *gifted* teacher is a blessing in any endeavor, including learning stand-up. A gifted teacher, knowledgeable in the techniques of writing and performing stand-up, will accelerate your development. Most important, a gifted teacher will help you find your own distinctive stand-up comedy voice.

The hallmarks of good teachers are:

- They have been instrumental in mentoring the careers of professional stand-ups
- You like them and you enjoy their classes
- You feel your work is noticeably improving as a result of their teaching
- You see that the work of your fellow students is improving
- You see that people in the class are developing their own distinctive comedy voices as opposed to just reproducing the way the teacher does stand-up
- If there is a final performance, it should go well for you and your classmates

Another venue for new stand-ups to try out material is an open mic. Most clubs have open mics. These are non-primetime events where anyone can get up and perform. In large cities like New York and Los Angeles, where stars and national headliners are performing every night of the year, people won't pay to see unknown stand-ups trying out new material. So at open mics in these cities, the audience may be composed entirely of the stand-ups waiting to perform. At open mics in smaller cities, however, paying audience members may be in attendance. It's important for you to figure out which situation you're in. An audience that includes paying customers is a more reliable gauge of new material than an audience made up exclusively of beginning comedians waiting to perform. Often other stand-ups are more focused on reviewing their own material than taking in a colleague's performance.

What many open mics lack, but a course or workshop includes, is the presence of a knowledgeable teacher. A good stand-up teacher will make sure that students are paying attention to each classmate's presentations rather than going over their own sets, as commonly occurs at open mics. A good teacher will have an ear for a joke that may not get laughs in class but might work in front of a paying club audience. Also, a good teacher will know when a joke that works in class won't work in a club. A good teacher also acts as the final arbiter of class feedback.

In the days before comedy clubs, stand-ups performed in nightclubs. People would go there to dance to the music of the house bands and see variety shows, which typically included musical acts, dancers, comedians, and novelty acts. In those days there was an adage passed down from the veteran stand-ups to the new guys in the circuit: **Don't play to the band.** What they meant was, don't try to crack up the guys in the band. Focus on getting laughs from the audience out front. Inside jokes can sometimes get big laughs from fellow performers but fall completely flat with the paying audience.

The same is true today. There are kinds of jokes that can get big laughs from fellow performers but no laughs from paying audiences. These are usually sexually graphic jokes. Or sometimes they're "jokey" jokes—by which I mean they clearly have nothing to do with the stand-up delivering them. Jokey jokes are generic, have no trace of believability, and can be told (maybe even have been told) by plenty of other people. They're almost certain to bomb with paying audiences. You don't score with a paying audience by being the filthiest, most generic and inauthentic stand-up they've ever seen. You score with them by being original, genuine, and funny.

At an open mic, in addition to the risk of getting laughs with unclubworthy material, there's the risk that good material won't get laughs. If you find yourself at an open mic where the other performers are your only audience, and they're looking at their show notes rather than watching what's happening onstage, and some of them are leaving after they've performed their set, you're not in a good place to gauge your material. Use the experience to get comfortable being onstage and using a microphone. If the vibe you're picking up from the other performers is "Let me do my thing and split," do not use their reaction or lack of reaction to determine what to keep, what to rewrite, or what to toss.

Some open mics are better than others. The good ones are usually produced by other stand-ups who set a good tone for the performance. They request that all the performers stay to the end of the lineup and pay attention to the comedians onstage instead of looking over their own material. If they offer feedback it's specific—a suggestion for how to rewrite a joke, for instance, or another way to perform it.

Always remember, however, that ultimately it's your decision whether to accept or reject feedback. Feedback should resonate with you; it should feel right. If it doesn't, reject it. The only feedback you cannot ignore is the laughter or absence of laughter that your jokes receive from paying audiences.

When receiving criticism and advice about your stand-up, it's important to consider the source. You want to pay the most attention to professional comedy people—people who make their living writing, performing, and/or producing comedy. Pay less attention to everyone else. And pay the least attention to people who have been striving for many years to establish themselves as comedy professionals but haven't succeeded.

I had a student who, after several productive workshops, performed at her first open mic. She was devastated by criticism she received there from another performer. She told me that he'd been doing open mics for over 10 years but made his living as a postman. Then she asked me, "Do you want to know what he said about my set?" I told her no. Anyone who's been at this for over 10 years and hasn't made it out of the open mic circuit clearly hasn't acquired the wisdom of the ages about stand-up comedy. I would eagerly take to heart anything this guy had to say about how many stamps to put on a package. But as for listening to his criticism of her stand-up, I told her, quoting Tony Soprano, "fuhgeddaboutit."

If you know other stand-ups who are doing open mics, get their recommendations for which are the best ones and which ones to avoid. Also, recommendations from stand-ups you admire can help you select the best stand-up comedy workshops and classes.

Comedy clubs also offer unknown stand-ups performance opportunities in shows they call "new talent nights." Stand-ups call them "bringer shows," because the performers are required to bring a certain number of paying customers in exchange for stage time. Typically, new stand-ups don't do these shows to try out first drafts; they wait until they have polished material. Their hope is that someone may be in attendance at these shows with the power to pluck them out of the amateur lineup and make them a paid pro. The odds that this will come true for you will improve when you get good, undeniably good, at writing and performing stand-up.

Besides performing at clubs, you can "create" audiences for your first draft by turning regular people into an audience. For instance, when one of my former students, the Emmy Award–winning comedy writer Ted Greenberg, was starting his career as a performer, after several distressing outings at open mics he started performing at Grand Central Station during the evening rush, when there were always commuters waiting for their trains. Ted found that this audience was a more accurate gauge of what would work in front of a club audience than the open mics. Several of my other students have performed in subways for the same reason. Parties are also great places to try out material. The hilarious "2000 Year Old Man" comedy albums by Mel Brooks and Carl Reiner were first performed and honed at parties where they were guests. You can try out first drafts in front of neighbors, friends, and colleagues. You can work jokes into your everyday conversations. When I'm writing comedy at home and see my neighbor Karl in his backyard, I go out and do the joke for him over the fence.

WARNING: If you turn regular people into an audience in the manner I just described, do not ask their opinion about your material. Just do it. Stand-up comedy is a subject lots of people think they know about. But in fact, it's a rare person who can read or hear a piece of stand-up comedy material and have a good sense of how it will play in front of a club audience. One student of mine tried out some new material in front of friends. They laughed throughout his material but then proceeded to tell him that, although the material was charming, it wasn't funny. Then why did they keep laughing? People can fake a laugh or two, but only well-trained actors can sustain fake laughter. If people laugh, the material is funny. That's all the useful information they have to give you.

Trying out your material in front of people will help you find the funny parts of your first draft. With this information in hand, you are prepared to take the next step in the writing process: formatting your material into setups and punchlines.

22

SETUP AND PUNCHLINE

THE BENCHMARK OF GREAT COMEDIANS is their capacity to get lots of big laughs. This has always been so, and so it will always remain. The silent-film star Charlie Chaplin is revered as one of the greatest, perhaps *the* greatest, comedian of all time. In an essay titled "Comedy's Greatest Era," the Pulitzer Prize–winning author, essayist, screenwriter, and critic James Agee wrote with unsurpassed insight into the work of Chaplin and the handful of other comedy geniuses who created a golden age of film comedy at the beginning of the 20th century. When Chaplin first appeared in movies, comedies were short films lasting from about 10 to 30 minutes. Here is Agee on Chaplin:

> Before Chaplin came to pictures, people were content with a couple of gags per comedy; he got some kind of laugh every second. The minute he began to work, he set standards—and continually forced them higher.

Stand-ups, because they use words and words take time to speak, can't get laughs every second. But they can get laughs every *few* seconds. A good example is Louis C.K.'s piece on playing Monopoly with his six-year-old daughter (see page 35). Once he establishes that she's too young to emotionally handle her inevitable loss, the laughter is nonstop. Another example was David Letterman's Top Ten List; he reliably got 10 laughs in under two minutes with this routine.

Because audiences are accustomed to hearing professional comedians get upwards of four laughs per minute, their ears are trained to expect this frequency of laughter when they're in a comedy club. This is not the case in alternative comedy rooms and in storytelling venues where the audience's expectation is to hear a compelling story or a provocative point of view.

But in comedy clubs and televised comedy shows, this audience expectation of frequent laughter is firmly in place, so stand-ups must concern themselves with their laughs-per-minute ratio. They typically shoot for an average of *at least four laughs per minute.*

This is accomplished by formatting comedy material into setups and punchlines. Setup and punchline is a format. Some new stand-ups confuse format with content: they believe setup and punchline jokes are inherently corny and cheesy, like the following:

Setup: Did you hear Cinderella got thrown off the basketball team?
Punchline: Yeah, she kept running away from the ball.

However, this is not the case. Virtually all stand-ups format their jokes into setup and punchline. Here, for example, is a smart and funny Jim Gaffigan joke:

Setup: I'm bald, blind, and pale.
Punchline: I'm like a gigantic recessive gene.

So let's break it down. The setup is the *essential* information the audience needs in order to get the punchline. I tell my students in class to underline the word <u>essential</u> in their notes, because the concept is so important. But since you've been good enough to buy my book, I've underlined it for you. Frankly, I'd feel more comfortable if you'd underline it again. Part of the art and craft of comedy writing is the ability to identify and eliminate words that aren't needed to get

the laugh. The first move a comedy writer makes to punch up a joke, then, is to shorten it. Below is a visual guideline.
If a setup is this long:

_____. That's a good setup.
If it's this long:

_____.

Still a good setup.
This long:

_____

_____. Still good.
If it's this long:

_____

_____

_____. It's OK.
If it's this long:

_____

_____

_____. It's OK, but
you're pushing it.
If it's even longer:

_____

_____

_____

_____

_____. It's too long. You need to rethink it.
There is one exception to this short-setup guideline. A long setup is justified when its purpose is to ratchet up tension that will pay off in a big laugh. For an example I have retooled a generic joke:

Setup: It's getting tough to have a conversation with my grandfather. He was telling me, "Your grandmother and I went to see this movie. It's a great movie, you have to see it. You can't miss this movie." "It sounds great, Grandpa, what's it called?" "What's it called? It's called. . . . It's red." (Frustrated that his grandson doesn't get what he's talking about) "It's red. It's almost always red, for God's sakes.

Come on, you know." "I'm sorry Grandpa, I don't understand."
(Grandpa's frustration is building) "How can you not understand!
It's red. It's got a stem. It has thorns. What's wrong with you?!"
(Grandson finally gets it) "Oh, a rose?" "Yes. Finally! Thank you."
Punchline: (Grandpa calling to his wife) "<u>Rose, what was the name
of that movie?</u>"

This laugh is set up by Grandpa's increasing frustration with his
grandson's inability to understand him. The audience has to see this
frustration building. Shortening the setup of this joke to a line or two
would kill the laugh.

If your long setup builds tension and pays off with a big laugh,
it's OK. If your joke doesn't require tension to set it up, keep it short.

The best technique for keeping setups short is to make sure they
contain only one subject. Rookies often don't know this and end up
creating overly long setups.

Here's an example of a newbie's setup:

I went to visit my parents last weekend [subject 1]. They're getting
kinda old [subject 2]. So I try to visit them as much as I can [sub-
ject 3]. They live out in Larchmont [subject 4]. It's a really pretty
town [subject 5]. It's right on the Long Island Sound [subject 6].
So last weekend was a family reunion [subject 7—no punchline
in sight]. So there were a lot of people there [subject 8]. And my
mother prepared a formal dinner [subject 9]. She gets really tense
when she cooks [subject 10]. And she makes everyone else really
tense [subject 11]. Part of what makes everybody so tense is that
she calls you out for less than perfect table manners [subject 12].

And, finally, the punchline:

So it ended up being a sit-up-straight dinner for twelve.

Here's the rewrite of that joke.

Setup: At dinner, my mother makes everybody tense by nagging them about proper table manners.
Punchline: Last night, she hosted a sit-up-straight dinner for twelve.

That's all the setup that joke needs. It doesn't matter how old Mom is, or how good a son or daughter you are, or where she lives, or what the town looks like. It doesn't matter what the occasion is, or whether she or somebody else cooked the dinner, or whether it was a formal or informal dinner. The only thing that's essential for the punchline to work is that Mom makes people tense at dinnertime by nagging them about their table manners. That's the subject of the joke, and that's all the setup needs to state.

If you go back and reread the "Rose" joke, you'll see that it, too, has a single subject: it's getting hard to talk with Grandpa. The words that follow need to be there because they show Grandpa's increasing frustration and annoyance with his grandson. The extraneous subjects in the "Sit up straight" joke do nothing to build tension or amplify the laugh. They should therefore be cut.

So, one attribute of a good setup is that it has one, and only one, subject.

In addition to clearly stating the subject, the setup needs to be clear about your feelings toward your subject. Remember, the real subject of your jokes is you. For example, doing jokes about rap music doesn't tell the audience much of anything about you. However, doing jokes about how you hate rap music—or adore it or are totally confused by it—makes your personality come alive to the audience.

Sometimes the emotion, or *attitude* as it's referred to in comedy, is stated explicitly: "I hate driving in the city." The subject is driving in the city and the attitude is, I hate it. Often the attitude doesn't need to be expressed in words, but can be clearly expressed through performance: (Alarmed) "My student debt!!!"

Most of the time people laugh because they're surprised by what is said in the punchline. So another feature of a good setup is that it protects the surprise of the punch. It misdirects the audience so they can't tell where you're going. If the audience can tell what your punch-line is before you deliver it, the laugh will be weak or nonexistent.

I worked with a Puerto Rican stand-up who in real life was a tough guy—genuinely intimidating—and that was manifest in his stand-up persona. Honestly, I felt empowered working with him. If someone greatly annoyed me and the thought crossed my mind, "Boy I wish that person would just disappear," I had a feeling that I was only one phone call away from making it happen. This stand-up, in real life, fell in love with a Chinese girl and they decided to marry. He had to meet her parents, who were immigrants from China. And like most immigrants, they were conservative in the sense that they hoped their daughter would marry a Chinese guy, ideally from their own province in China, and that he'd be a doctor or an MIT professor. So the couple knew that introducing her parents to their future son-in-law, a scary-looking Puerto Rican stand-up comic, was not going to trigger a champagne toast. We wrote jokes that conveyed this:

Setup: I couldn't believe it: the moment I walk into the room her father starts pointing at me and yelling, "I know you! I know you! You mugged me! You mugged me!"
Punchline: I can't believe (slight pause) he remembered that.

In summation, here are the attributes of a good setup:

- It is concise
- It is clear about its single subject
- It is clear about your attitude toward the subject
- It leads directly to a punchline
- It protects the surprise of the punchline

Now let's examine the punchline.

The punchline is what triggers the laugh. Usually in stand-up it's expressed in words. But it can also be a facial expression, or a piece of physical comedy, or a sound effect. The word *punchline* is advice to you from your foremothers and forefathers in comedy. It's instructing you to punch the laugh line, to emphasize it vocally, to make it clear to the audience when they're expected to laugh.

A punchline needs to be short. The second the audience gets the joke, they want to laugh. If your punchline continues after the audience gets the joke, you're stepping on your laugh and you may kill it. It's easy to rectify this situation. End the punchline where the audience laughs. So, for example, the original punchline of Kate Redway's joke about not going to church because "all they read is the Bible" was "I already read that. Can't they read something else, for Chrissake?!" (See page 74.) After the audience showed us by their laughter exactly where the laugh was, we cut the second sentence.

A punchline usually needs to be a surprise. Often this surprise is created by an unexpected shift in attitude from the setup to the punchline. A good example is arguably the best-known punchline in American history: Henny Youngman's "Take my wife—please." He usually performed it as a one-liner, but it worked best when he added a short setup. I saw him perform the joke in the '60s, a time when the role of women in society was changing dramatically. More women were going to college and graduate school and getting full-time jobs and building careers, and fewer women were staying home to be full-time wives and moms. Here's how Henny delivered the joke:

*Women have really changed today. Take my wife—*please.

The italicized words are the setup. The punchline is one word: "please."

Youngman's attitude on the setup was "impressed." Something big and historic was taking place in society. You expected him to say something like "Women have really changed today. Take my wife. She just graduated from NYU Business School and got a big job with an accounting firm!" However, at the one-word punchline the attitude—impressed—abruptly shifts to one of desperation and panic. If someone in the audience doesn't bail this man out of his marriage tonight, he may not make it till the morning. This sudden shift in attitude creates the comic surprise.

Let's review. A good punchline is

- Concise
- Comes as a surprise
- Clearly expresses your attitude

There's an important variation of the setup and punchline format. It's called a *roll*. A roll is a setup followed by multiple punchlines, all of which key off the one setup. Letterman's Top Ten List was a roll. The setup was the list's subject: "Here are 10 reasons why . . ." And each of the 10 reasons was a punchline. Louis C.K.'s "Monopoly" piece is also a roll. Once he sets it up by saying that his six-year-old isn't mature enough to handle the dark and heavy loss in Monopoly, it is punch, punch, punch. He gets 14 laughs in the first minute of this piece. The comedic power of a roll stems from its capacity to have one laugh follow the next without interruption.

Laughter creates laughter. If you walk into a room where people are laughing heartily, you start to smile even though you don't know *why* they're laughing. Part of the art and craft of comedy writing is learning not to get in the way of the laughter. Rolls, by having a single setup with multiple punchlines, are a great way to accomplish this.

Two ways of helping you write rolls is to conceptualize them as either a *list roll* or an *act-out roll*.

The Top Ten List is a list roll that draws attention to the fact that it's a list. But this needn't be the case. I had a student who was dating a veterinarian. We created a list roll about his struggles with her. Though it was structured as a list, the audience didn't hear it that way. They heard it as a story about his relationship:

Setup: So I'm dating this veterinarian and I don't think it's going to work out.

Punch 1: When she's annoyed at me, she rolls up a newspaper and <u>smacks me on the nose</u>.

Punch 2: When she wants to get romantic she says to me, <u>"Sit!"</u>

Punch 3: <u>"Stay."</u>

Punch 4: <u>"Roll over."</u>

Louis C.K.'s "Monopoly" piece is a good example of an act-out roll. Here's how it looks when broken down into its setup and punches:

Setup: I play Monopoly with my kids; that's really fun. My nine-year-old, she can totally do Monopoly. The six-year-old actually totally gets how the game works, but she's not emotionally developed enough to handle her <u>inevitable loss</u>

Punch 1: <u>in every game of Monopoly.</u>

Punch 2: Because the Monopoly loss <u>is dark,</u>

Punch 3: <u>it's heavy.</u>

Punch 4: It's not like when you lose at, you know, Candy Land: "Ohh, you got stuck <u>in the fudgy thing, baby!</u>

Punch 5: Oh well, you're <u>in the gummy twirly o's and you didn't get to win.</u>"

Punch 6: But when she loses in Monopoly I gotta look at her little face and I go . . . "OK, so here's what's going <u>to happen now, OK?</u>

Punch 7: <u>All your property . . .</u>

Punch 8: <u>everything you have</u>

Punch 9: . . . all your railroads, your houses, all your money . . . <u>that's mine now.</u>

Punch 10: Gotta give it all to me. <u>Give it to me.</u>

Punch 11: <u>That's right.</u>

Punch 12: And no, no you <u>can't play anymore, see,</u>

Punch 13: because even though you're giving me all of that? It doesn't even touch how <u>much you owe me.</u>

Punch 14: <u>Doesn't even touch it, baby.</u>

Punch 15: You're going down hard, <u>it's really bad.</u>

Punch 16: <u>All you've been working</u> for all day,

Punch 17: <u>I'm gonna take it now</u> . . .

Punch 18: and I'm going to use it to <u>destroy your sister.</u>

Punch 19: I mean I'm gonna <u>ruin her.</u>

Punch 20: It's just <u>mayhem on this board for her now.</u>"

Here's an assignment: Write a roll with a setup that is followed by at least 3 punches—5 is better, 10 is superb, but 3 is a good start.

A hundred years ago, Charlie Chaplin delivered lots of big laughs to his audience. Louis C.K. does it today. Now it's your turn. Setup and punchline and rolls are the formats that will enable you to achieve this hallmark of a master comedian.

23

WORKING BACKWARD

AFTER YOU'VE TRIED OUT YOUR FIRST DRAFT, you need to work backward in order to format the material into setup and punchline jokes. Your tryout audience will give you an idea of where the laughs are in your first draft. With this information, you work backward from the line (or facial expression or gesture or sound effect) that got the laugh to the beginning of the joke. Knowing where your punchline is enables you to write a concise setup.

In your first draft, you may have lines that aren't necessary for either your setup or your punchline. In this second draft, you're going to delete these lines. (They are deleted from the joke, but not necessarily thrown away. Many good comedy writers don't discard what they've edited out of their first draft. At a later date they may revisit this material and find something funny in it they can use for a new joke.) The only words that remain in this second draft are the ones essential to the joke's setup and punchline. This process of working backward helps you create clear, tightly written setups and multiple punchlines.

To clarify the process of working backward, let's take another look at Laura Bassi's first draft. The underlines indicate where the tryout audience laughed.

Everyone tries to teach their kids animal sounds because it's cute,
but half the sounds aren't even what the animals say . . . What
does the cow say? Moo? Umm, like, why is that a thing we teach
kids? No animal sounds like that. You don't go to a zoo and hear
the pigs going oink oink . . . you hear them and they're like (makes
real pig sound) and no one wants their children walking around
doing that noise. We should really approach it from a different
angle, like, "What do pigs think?" And the answer is "Please don't
slaughter me into tiny pieces, then reprocess me into that lunch-
meat ham you love on your deli sandwiches." This doesn't help
them with their life. Let's help them. Sometimes men are pigs. So
what do pigs say? "Dang, girl, you look good; come over here."
Why not use this format to teach them other things so they know
what to do with their lives: What does the twenty-seven-year-old
with no career who is taking care of you right now say? "HELP!!"

Once Laura identified where the laughs were, she worked backward
to create the setups. Laura making the real pig sound was the first laugh.
So she realized that the cow line could go, and so could the subject of
why parents teach this stuff to kids. The subject that was needed to set
up her first laugh was that the animal sounds we teach kids are bogus.
Here's the rewrite:

Setup: Everyone tries to teach their kids animal sounds because
    it's cute, but half the sounds aren't even what the animals
    say . . . "Pigs say OINK!" Pigs don't say OINK. Pigs say:
Punchline 1: (Laura makes real pig noise.)

Setup: That's not cute. No one wants their child walking around going:
Punchline 1: (Laura repeats pig noises.)

The next laugh was the line "Dang, girl, you look good; come
over here." Knowing this, she was able to eliminate all of the language
about the subject *What do pigs think?* and move on to the subject
that sets up the next laugh: *Sometimes men are pigs.*

Setup: Sometimes men are pigs, so what do pigs say?
Punchline 1: "Dang, girl, you look good. Come over here!"

This rewrite enabled Laura to tighten the joke by eliminating language that didn't contribute to a laugh. Further, by clarifying the subject of this joke, she was able to add an additional punch:

Punchline 2: "Hey, I'm super-drunk and not ready for a relationship. You wanna come over?"

The next laugh was Laura's "HELP!!" She decided that her first-draft setup made the subject clear, so she retained it. The clarity of the subject enabled her to come up with a second punch:

Setup: Why not use this format to teach them other things so they know what to do with their lives? Like what does the twenty-seven-year-old with no career who is taking care of you right now say?
Punchline 1: "HELP!!"
Punchline 2: "Don't ever major in communications!"

By working backward, Laura streamlined her rambling first draft into more tightly and clearly written setup and punchline jokes. This process enabled her to:

- Identify the subject of the laugh line and cut out the words that were extraneous to this subject, thus tightening the joke
- Cut out all the words that were extraneous to the punchline, further tightening the joke
- Add more punchlines once her setup was clarified

Sometimes in the process of streamlining a joke, you cut words that are essential to the joke and, in so doing, damage it. An example of this is a joke written by a student of mine, Rosco Nash. It is a joke about his six-year-old daughter losing her teeth:

My six-year-old is at the age where her body is changing and growing so fast. It's like overnight she lost three front teeth on the top and three front teeth on the bottom. She looks like a midget meth head. I'm saying to my wife, "Did we take all the Sudafed or is Ruby smoking it?"

Rosco got a suggestion to cut the opening words about his daughter's growth spurts. The idea was that the only essential information the joke required was that her teeth fell out. The suggested rewritten joke would start with, "My daughter lost three front teeth on the top and three front teeth on the bottom."

This was not a good suggestion. A setup needs to be clear about the subject and also clear about how you feel toward the subject. The suggested cut would have made Rosco's attitude toward his daughter's missing teeth unclear. Without the original opening words, it could seem like Rosco was ridiculing his daughter's looks, which was not his intention. If the audience thought it was his intention, they would think he was a schmuck. His intention was to express his astonishment at how fast she is growing. The joke as originally written was a loving father's comic observation. The proposed cut would have upended his intention, damaged his likability, and, in so doing, weakened if not killed the laugh.

If you tighten up the writing of a joke and it gets less of a laugh than the original did, restore the cut words. You need them.

Now it's your turn. Begin by underlining the places in your first draft where you got laughs from your tryout audience. Remember to be generous in your assessment of what constitutes a laugh. Later on, once you've performed the material in front of a club audience, the standards for a laugh will go way up. A real club audience will be the most accurate gauge of your material. How they react over the course of a few performances will determine which jokes stay, which jokes go, and which jokes need punching up. At this earlier stage, you don't want to make the mistake of cutting material that may, with a little more work, get strong laughs. So be an easy grader.

24

CREATING YOUR SET LIST

ONCE YOU'VE FORMATTED YOUR MATERIAL into setup and punchline jokes, you're ready to create your set list. A set list is the order in which you'll perform your jokes.

There are several factors to consider in selecting your opening jokes. It's important to get one or two solid laughs within the first 30 seconds of your set. Every time a new stand-up takes the stage, there's a question in the audience's mind: *Is this person funny?* You want to answer that question as quickly as possible. When you get one or two "A" laughs at the outset of your routine, the audience makes up its mind: *She's good! She's funny!* Once this matter is settled, they'll cut you some slack if a few jokes down the line don't get laughs. It's also important for *you* to hear those laughs at the outset of your performance. The big worry always is *Will I get laughs?* Hearing that reassuring sound of laughter rolling in from the audience right at the beginning of your set puts that worry to rest.

But you don't want to start with your absolute best jokes. You want to save those jokes for the end, so that your act builds and you leave the stage in glory, with gales of laughter. So you want to start with your second-strongest jokes and end with your strongest.

If you're just starting out and have never performed at a club before, you'll need to make an educated guess about the relative comic firepower of your jokes. You won't know for sure until you've tried the jokes out several times in front of an audience (a paying one, preferably). For now, make your best guess. After you have some stage time under your belt, you won't be guessing anymore.

If there is some feature of you that is salient—you have an exotic name; you're extremely tall or short, fat or thin; or, as was the case with several of my students, you are blind, deaf, missing a limb, or have some other visible physical impairment—and you have jokes about it, it's good to start with these jokes. They're a good way to make an instant connection with your audience. If the feature is extremely obvious, something so noticeable that the audience is going to focus on it the moment you get onstage, you *need* to have opening jokes about it—because if you don't, that's all the audience is going to be thinking about throughout your performance. But if you do, they'll soon be ready for you to move on to other subjects. So, for example, in his opening joke my one-armed student complimented the stand-up who went before him and said:

Wow, wasn't Craig great?! <u>Let's give him another hand. (Holds up his one hand.)</u>

You want your audience to get who you are, right up front. You want to be a vivid presence onstage. So another factor in determining which jokes to open with is to identify the ones that establish your comic personality. The more you write and perform, the clearer your comic personality will become. (Chapter 34, "Creating Your Persona," will explain how the process works.)

Here's an example of opening material that gives the audience a clear picture of the stand-up's comic personality. The stand-up is a student of mine, Aise O'Neil. What you need to know about him is that he's young—a high school sophomore—very tall and thin, and has long hair that sometimes covers his eyes. His persona builds off of his looks. He comes across as smart and socially awkward. Here's how he opens his set:

When I was younger, I used to go to summer camp a lot. Then I told my parents I hated it. They asked me why and I said, well . . . the hygiene, the food, the people, the activities, the accommodation, the area, the heat, the fact that it's a Jewish camp and we're not Jewish, and some other reasons . . . such as the counselors, the staff, the employees, the other campers, the poor laundry service. Did I mention the food? The inadequate medical facilities, the nurses, the insects, the bus rides, the fact that no phones are allowed which is a bit suspicious because it makes you think they're hiding something, camping out, camp fires, camp songs, no nuts are allowed. So I don't go to camp anymore. I go to therapy.

These opening jokes clearly establish Aise's persona. They enable him to connect with the audience, because he clearly doesn't look like a boy who enjoys outdoor life. Also, with these jokes, he fulfills the requirement of getting laughs early on. The routine is a list roll; the subject of his setup is explaining to his parents why he doesn't like camp. The setup is followed by 20 consecutive punches.

There are certain jokes that don't do well up front—for example, jokes about sex and your sex life. When we're looking at jokes on a page, it's easy to forget that introducing yourself to a club audience is a social situation. If you were meeting people in a social situation outside of a club and while extending your hand for the introductory handshake you said, "So I was jerking off earlier and . . ." there would be several reasons at least why your hand might go unshaken.

If you want to be edgy or shocking up front, keep in mind that you have to take the audience with you. They have to like you to go along with your edgy material. You don't want material up front that pushes the audience away from you.

It's possible to shock an audience and delight them. I want to give you an example that requires some explanation. It was the opening joke of an African American student of mine in a showcase performance at Carolines in the late 1980s. Back then, although there were African American superstars in stand-up like Richard Pryor and Eddie

Murphy, the lower tiers of stand-up were overwhelmingly dominated by white men. It was rare to see a black stand-up in a showcase of new comedians. And for that reason it was rare to see African Americans in the audience. A new black stand-up at a comedy club in those days often performed in front of a sea of white faces. Sometimes this would put both performer and audience on edge. My student wanted to connect with this feeling of unease. His salient feature was the simple fact that he, an African American, was in the showcase. He made his entrance at Carolines with a smile on his face and delivered this opening line with warmth and friendship to his all-white audience:

Hey! Did you ever kill anybody by mistake?

It was an edgy joke in that it gave voice to a negative stereotype some white people harbor about African American people being violent. It was delivered right up front and got a huge laugh. By comically acknowledging this bigoted thought that some people harbor, this stand-up forged an instant rapport with his white audience.

Let's review the attributes you're looking for in your opening jokes:

- They get one or two big laughs within the first 30 seconds or so
- They give the audience a picture of your comic personality
- They acknowledge your salient feature, if you have one
- They can be edgy and shocking but shouldn't make your audience feel uncomfortable with you
- They should leave the audience looking forward to what you next have to say

Now let's go to the back end of your set list. You want to end with your best jokes. An insight into the importance of a stand-up's final jokes was imparted to me by Jack Rollins, the legendary comedy manager and producer whose clients included Nichols and May, Robin Williams, Billy Crystal, David Letterman, Woody Allen, Martin Short. He said, "What's most important is not that an audience remembers your jokes. What's most important is that they remember you." The last impression you leave with your audience has a lot to do with whether or not they'll want to see you again. So finish with your strongest jokes. Again, if you're just starting out, make your best guess about which of your jokes these might be. Once you start performing with some regularity you'll be able to make this decision based on your experience and not on guesswork.

Once you've chosen your beginning and end jokes, here's how to plan which jokes go in the middle.

If you're planning on doing crowd work, the middle of your set is usually the best place for it. Crowd work does best after you've made the audience trust you and like you through your opening jokes. Once you've established a rapport, they feel safe participating in your act. And this rapport also gives you the license to take risks. That's why established stand-ups try out new material in the middle of their sets.

In all likelihood, even at the very beginning of your stand-up career you'll have several jokes on the same subject—dating, for example. You'll also probably have several jokes on a completely different subject, such as your family. And you may have, say, some celebrity put-down jokes that have nothing to do with any of your other subjects. The jokes on the same subject naturally cluster together. Putting together jokes that share the same subject will help you shape the middle section of your set.

Sometimes your opening jokes may perfectly tee up a cluster of middle jokes. For example, if your opening jokes are about recently breaking up with your boyfriend or girlfriend, it would be good to follow these jokes with your dating jokes. And some of your middle cluster jokes may perfectly tee up your final jokes. For instance, if your closers are jokes about what it must be like to be Donald Trump's kids, it would be good to precede those jokes with the middle cluster jokes about your own family.

But what do you do when, for instance, you've come to the end of your cluster of family jokes and you want to start your celebrity put-down jokes and they have nothing to do with each other? It's time, then, to figure out how you can go from a cluster of jokes on one subject to a cluster of jokes on a completely unrelated subject.

Now, I could have written, "how you *transition* from a cluster of jokes on one subject to . . ." etc. I didn't, because you *shouldn't* transition from one joke subject to the next. I'll explain.

When you're writing an essay, it must be clear how one idea leads to the next, how one subject connects to the next subject, and so on. Transitions are useful and important in expository writing as ways to connect two related subjects. Your stand-up routine, however, is not an essay on a single thesis that is made up of interrelated subjects and opinions. Your routine is a piece of entertainment that may span many subjects that have nothing in common. The only thing that holds them together is the fact that *you* are saying them. That's what's important. In stand-up, **you are the transition. It is your comic personality that ultimately links together all of your jokes.**

No comedian understands this better than Steven Wright. Here he is on a variety of subjects that seemingly have nothing to do with each other:

> I used to be a narrator for <u>bad mimes</u>. I was walking through the forest alone and a tree fell right in front of me and <u>I didn't hear it</u>. <u>Are there any questions?</u> <u>Feeling kinda hyper.</u> Went to the hardware store, bought some <u>used paint</u>. It was in the <u>shape of a house</u>. I also bought some batteries, <u>but they weren't included</u>. So I had <u>to buy them again</u>.

It would be pointless and confusing to try to make transitions between these jokes. Steven Wright would never say, "I used to be a narrator for bad mimes. Mimes work alone, and speaking of being alone, I was walking through a forest alone and a tree fell right in front of me and I didn't hear it." His seemingly random remarks are all tied together not by transitions but by his personality. This is a man who is clearly marching to the beat of a different drummer.

Jimmy Fallon is not an eccentric character comedian like Steven Wright. He's the guy we'd love to have a beer with, the guy we'd love to have as a friend. But like Steven Wright, as well as the hosts of late-night TV talk shows who came before him, Fallon's opening stand-up monologues eschew transitions. For instance:

> Here's some celebrity news. There's talk that LeBron James's mother is dating a rapper. It got awkward when her boyfriend was like, "Wait, you have a kid?" (He dances.) Hey are you guys using Vine? Forty people, I love it. I use Vine, it's fun. I use it, it's pretty cool—you post, like, short little videos on this app. Well, I just read about this guy, he posted a six-second video of his breakup. Which he felt pretty good about, until his girlfriend said, "That's not the only six-second video we made." Hey ladies, here's some really good news for you: A new study around the world found that women are living longer than ever. While they haven't said why, I've started eating Luna Bars just in case.

Fallon moves from the subject of LeBron James's mother dating a rapper, to the subject of the Vine app, to the subject of women living longer than men, without any transitions. This doesn't confuse the audience; they are accustomed to comedians going from one subject to another without explanation or transition.

In fact, trying to manufacture a segue that ties together two unrelated jokes can confuse an audience; it makes them not quite sure what you're talking about. Remember that a good setup has only one subject. Furthermore, writing transitions creates more language that won't get laughs, hurting your laughs-per-minute ratio. If, however, the segue itself contains a laugh, then by all means keep it in. For example:

> Donald Trump said that his recent trip to Mexico was positive and constructive. The Mexican people had a slightly different take. According to the papers, it was the biggest disaster in

<u>Mexican history</u>. Speaking of disasters of historic proportions, <u>I had a date last night</u>. . . .

You want your set to have a good flow. That isn't achieved by artificially linking together jokes that have different subjects. In performance, you'll learn that certain jokes tee up other jokes even though they have different subjects. You'll also learn that some jokes are good openers, some are good closers, and some are good in between. And you'll learn how to order your jokes so that your act starts strong and builds from there to a big finish. This knowledge, gained by experience, will enable you over time to create a set that has an organic, natural flow.

OK, so now you have setup and punchline jokes ordered into a well-constructed set list. It's time to turn our attention to performing stand-up comedy.

Part IV

THE HANDBOOK
FOR PERFORMING
STAND-UP COMEDY

25

NERVES AND THE THREE GIFTS THEY GIVE YOU

DOES THE THOUGHT OF DOING STAND-UP make you nervous? If so, that says something about you. It says that you are a certifiably sane and rational human being. There are certain endeavors that *should* make a sentient person nervous, and doing stand-up comedy has got to be at the top of the list.

Year after year in opinion polls, people say that their number-one fear is public speaking. They fear that more than death. As Jerry Seinfeld put it:

> This means to the average person, if you have to be at a funeral, you would rather be in the casket than doing the eulogy.

Now that we've established that at first you may get nervous doing stand-up, please don't put this book down and look for one on *How to Become a Dental Hygienist* or *Your Future in Reupholstery*. The idea that you might get nervous isn't bad news—it's good news. Consider this: When I started my workshop, I noticed something surprising happening time and time again: my students' first performances tended to be among the very best they gave early in their development. Stand-up debuts seemed to be blessed by the comedy gods. I wondered why.

I learned that a big contributing factor was nerves. When you're onstage, your nerves do three things for you that are not just helpful to you as a performer, they are essential.

The first gift your nerves give you is energy. I can make you this guarantee: if you don't get a jot of sleep the night before your debut, when you hear the MC say, "Please welcome to the stage our next performer . . ." and then he says your name and the audience starts applauding, you may feel many things at that moment but *tired* will not be one of them.

Energy onstage is essential for a performer. Your energy stimulates the audience and enables you to dominate the room. Low-energy, listless performers bore their audiences.

Here's a second guarantee: When you get on the stage and start speaking, your mind will not wander. You are not going to drift off into thoughts of possible snack options for after the show. All your faculties will be totally focused on connecting with your audience and doing your act just as you rehearsed it. That's the second gift your nerves will give you: an exceptional ability to focus on your performance and connect with your audience. Here is Louis C.K. on the subject of these first two gifts:

> I get antsy. I don't like waiting to go onstage. I get very anxious and it's just uncomfortable. I learned that it's important to seize on that instead of running away from it. So I stay in the back and bottle up the energy so that when I go onstage I'm more connected.

Something comforting to know about your nerves is that people don't see them. Often in my workshop, a comedian who was performing just a few feet from the audience will sit down after a terrific set and tell us he or she was a nervous wreck up there. But none of us knew it or saw it. We didn't see it because the usual things your nerves do to you are invisible to an audience. The audience can't see sweaty palms, or butterflies in your stomach. And if you get sweat stains, you wear a sweater or a jacket. If your hands shake, you leave the microphone in the stand.

Besides, audiences aren't looking for signs of nervousness in a performer. They don't go to comedy clubs for that. They're there to enjoy the comedy. And when your set opens with two strong laughs, as we talked about in the last chapter, they start to laugh right away. They're having fun. They're focused on your comedy, not your sweat glands.

To help you understand this, let's look at another form of live entertainment: music. Let's say you're at a concert featuring the Stones or Radiohead or Bruce Springsteen or Arcade Fire or whoever is your favorite. The opening chords of the first song are sounded. The performers launch into their music. Are you sitting there wondering whether or not they're nervous? Of course not. You're focused on enjoying their music. Likewise, your comedy club audience is focused on enjoying your stand-up.

Audiences can, however, clearly see a positive manifestation of your nerves: your excitement about being onstage. That they see. **And the ability to communicate to your audience, "I am so excited to be up here talking to you," is the single most important part of performing stand-up** and the third gift your nerves give you.

When you start performing stand-up with some frequency, there will be times when you *don't* feel nervous. If the producer puts you up at the very end of a long show, and most of the audience has already gone, and there's only one occupied table left, and you've noticed that everyone at that table is talking loudly in Korean, you may not feel nervous. In that case, it will take technique to communicate to them you're having a ball talking to them and there's no place on Earth you'd rather be other than with them.

But in the beginning of your career, you won't need technique to convey your excitement about being onstage. That will come through loud and clear, courtesy of your nerves.

People have trouble performing when they misunderstand their nerves. They see their nerves as a sign that something terrible is happening. In fact, the opposite is true: something normal and good is happening.

Your nerves will give you the energy and concentration you need to do your best onstage. Further, the audience will not see the part of your nerves that are unsettling to you. The only part they see is your excitement about being with them and doing what you have always dreamed of doing—making them laugh. And they will love you for it.

Your nerves are a gift. Trust them.

26

THE SINGLE MOST IMPORTANT THING: JOYOUS COMMUNICATION

JOYOUS COMMUNICATION IS THE SINGLE most important technique in performing stand-up comedy. Joyous communication does not mean you're communicating how joyous you feel. Happiness is a wonderful thing to experience in life, but it is not funny. It's hard to get a laugh on how great things are going for you. What joyous communication means is that you take joy in communicating to the audience your emotions, be they anger, confusion, outrage, excitement, frustration, love, or whatever else you're feeling.

You've probably already experienced joyous communication, though perhaps not onstage. When something really annoying happens to you, you probably have someone in your life you can't wait to tell about it: "You will not believe what that SOB said to me . . ." or "So after waiting in line forever, I finally get to the window and the idiot behind the desk says to me . . ." That feeling that you have when you get to unload to a sympathetic listener—that is joyous communication.

Here's why it's of the utmost importance for entertainers.

When individuals come together to form an audience, something transformational takes place. Soon after the show starts and people start laughing, the emotional weather system in the room changes. People catch each other's eyes and smile at each other, mutually acknowledging their pleasure in the performance. A cold room of strangers, some of whom may have been fighting each other for parking spaces before the show, has become a warm room of friends and acquaintances. Who is responsible for this?

The performer, that's who. Here is how this is accomplished.

People in the audience are sitting in the dark, facing you, the performer. You and you alone are in the light. You are above them on a stage, so they can all see you clearly. All eyes are focused on you. You are the center of their attention. As a result, the individuals in the audience stop feeling what they were feeling before the show—*I'm nervous about getting that report done by Thursday . . . Why the hell does my wife always pick the most expensive lot to park the car? . . . I'm excited about starting vacation*—and start feeling what you are feeling.

That's why joyous communication is so important. If you communicate to your audience the feeling *There's no place on Earth I would rather be than right here on this stage talking to you. Thank God you're here!* your audience will feel *Thank God I'm here with this comedian. I'm loving this guy.*

On the other hand if you communicate, *Let me get this thing over with so I can get out of here,* your audience will feel, *When is this guy going to get this thing over with and get off the stage?*

Obviously, that's not the whole ballgame. You also need funny material, and you need to perform it skillfully. But unless you have a deadpan persona like Steven Wright, performing your material without joyous communication makes it unlikely that you will kill.

Let me give you what was for me an unforgettable example, though it involved a pop star, not a comedian. When I was in grad school, Laura Nyro performed on campus. The venue was large—Memorial Auditorium at Stanford University—and it was packed with her adoring fans.

She came onstage to thunderous applause. She sat at the piano and began singing and playing her hit songs, beautifully. If you closed your eyes it sounded like her records: she was that perfect. When she finished a song, she would stare at the keyboard and wait for our applause to subside and then start the next song. She never acknowledged our presence. She wasn't playing for us. She was waiting for us to finish applauding so she could start the next song. The applause between songs diminished; we didn't want to hold her up. When she finished playing her repertoire—to perfection—she got up, nodded toward the audience, and left the stage, to tepid applause. Her superb musicianship couldn't compensate for her utter indifference toward the audience. It was clear she didn't want to be there, and by the end of the concert, neither did her audience.

Now let's take an example from the opposite end of the entertainment spectrum: a beginning student of mine who was completely unfunny. This is a rarity; almost everyone has some sense of humor, but this guy was a humor-free zone. And for some unfathomable reason he loved doing stand-up comedy. He adored it.

He'd get up in front of the class and have a blast talking to us. You could tell this wasn't just the high point of his day; it was the high point of his life. He'd beam at us and we'd beam back at him. When he was done, we'd applaud him enthusiastically. You couldn't help liking this guy, because he so clearly enjoyed being with us. Nobody laughed at his jokes; he wasn't funny. Even when I wrote some good jokes for him, he'd change them in just precisely the right way to kill them. But we enjoyed our time with him.

Then came his performance at Carolines on Broadway. Now, you would think that if you'd been in a stand-up-comedy workshop for several weeks and had distinguished yourself by being the only student never to get a single laugh, you might be a tad apprehensive about performing in what at the time was the most important comedy club in New York. Not him.

He didn't walk onstage—he bounded. He wasn't terrified, which would have been sensible under the circumstances. He was thrilled to be on that stage. If Carolines was the Yankee Stadium of comedy, its audience was looking at a rookie striding to the plate with the swagger of a Babe Ruth.

He radiated joyous communication, and as a result he told his jokes to a sea of smiling faces. Nobody laughed. He wasn't funny. But when he finished striking out, he was greeted with enthusiastic applause from an audience who had enjoyed their time with him because he had adored his time with them.

Unfortunately for this plucky fellow, audiences don't go to clubs to smile; they go to laugh. There's no future in comedy for the chronically unfunny. Yet for his five minutes in the big leagues he held the audience at Carolines in the palm of his hands and won their affection to a degree that Laura Nyro, with all her fame and supreme talent, didn't achieve that night at Stanford.

When you add artistry to joyous communication, you get a great performer. A performer who has talent but lacks joyous communication may be admirable but ultimately in a live performance is a stage weight.

But what happens if you're in a bad mood? What happens if, just as you're being introduced, thoughts like these are going through your head? *My as-of-yesterday ex-girlfriend just called me and told me I left something at her place, and when I asked, "What is it?" she tells me that in about seven months it will be either a girl or a boy. And now the MC is introducing me and he's doing a lame joke at my expense. And the audience is laughing at me and this frigging moron just mispronounced my name!!! I'm not feeling the joyous communication! What do I do now, Yoda?*

First of all, let me acknowledge you're having a really bad day. There is an answer to your question. It lies in a simple truth that is the basis of cognitive therapy: your thoughts influence your moods.

If you are thinking frightening thoughts, you will *feel* frightened. *They're going to hate me. I'm not going to get any laughs. My material stinks.* Thoughts like these will produce fear in you. And you don't want to be terrified while you're onstage doing comedy.

If, on the other hand, you are thinking realistic, positive thoughts, you will feel good. *I've really honed my material. It's been working well. I've been getting laughs. The more I'm onstage the better I get at this. I'm getting to do what I love doing most—giving people laughter.* Please note these are realistic, positive thoughts, not fanciful ones— which is an important distinction. Because if you're thinking, *I'm the greatest. They're going to roar with laughter at everything I say. I'm going to get a standing ovation!*—these are fanciful, delusional thoughts that will tee you up for failure more certainly than doing 20 minutes of how-you-wipe-yourself jokes.

Focusing your mind on realistic, positive thoughts will enable you to consistently enter the emotional sweet spot that is joyous communication. Make it an essential part of your warmup. When you're up next, consciously think this: *I'm going to go out there and have a great time talking to these people.* Make it your mantra.

Don't wait for the audience to show you affection. Bring the affection onstage with you, and because they feel what you feel, they will give it back to you in return.

Your time onstage can be a sanctuary for you. It can be a time and place to set aside sadness, anger, and anxiety. During those minutes of stage time, you can experience that heightened sense of living that comes with the lights, the laughter, the applause.

Here's an assignment that will enable you to see clearly what I mean by all this: Watch any episode of Louis C.K.'s show *Louie*. In every episode, Louis struggles with angst involving either his kids, his ex-wife, his girlfriend, or his career. There's only one time when we consistently see Louis having a great time—when he's performing his stand-up at the Comedy Cellar. When you look at his face, you are seeing joyous communication.

Before each show I produce, I gather together my new students and ask them, "What's the most important thing tonight?" Sometimes they reply, "Get laughs" or "Remember my jokes" or "Hold for my laughs." But because they're good students, they usually give the right answer: "Have fun!"

Sustain joyous communication throughout your performance and you will see in front of you people who are laughing at your jokes and, between laughs, smiling with the pleasure that comes from being with someone who loves being with them.

27

COMING ALIVE ONSTAGE: EMOTIONAL FULLNESS

WHEN WE THINK OF FAMOUS COMEDIANS, we can picture how they'd act in situations that we haven't actually seen them in. If we imagine them at a party, for instance, the life of the party would be Jimmy Fallon. He'd be singing and dancing, telling jokes, laughing uproariously at other peoples' jokes, and organizing parlor games. Louis C.K. would be off in a corner, drinking a beer, trying not to talk to anyone. Because she's so adorable, Sarah Silverman would have a circle of guys around her, but they'd peel off one by one as she unknowingly insulted their race, religion, ethnicity, or sexual orientation. She wouldn't notice anything was wrong. Around Lisa Lampanelli there would be a large circle of men and women of all sorts, laughing as she *knowingly* insulted each of them. Lewis Black would be passionately talking politics and would get so upset about the day's news that someone would have to light his cigarette for him since his hands would be shaking so badly. People at the party would think Gilbert Gottfried was there because his is the loudest voice in the room. In fact, he wasn't invited; he's just somewhere in the neighborhood.

Gifted comedians create a distinct comic persona; they're so clear about who they are that we feel we really know them. When I was a little boy I was convinced that the great comedian Jack Benny, whom I saw on television every week, was my uncle.

Creating a persona takes time; it takes many, many performances, usually over the course of several years, to crystallize who you are as a stand-up. However, you can get this process off to a strong start right at the outset of your stand-up career. The key is learning to be *emotionally full* onstage.

Being emotionally full means that the audience knows moment to moment how you feel about what you're saying. It doesn't mean that you're expressing your feelings loudly. It means you're expressing them clearly. Your way of expressing feelings will help define who you are to your audiences. For example, Gilbert Gottfried, Jessica Kirson, and Don Rickles have an explosive way of expressing their feelings. David Letterman's way is sardonic. Bob Newhart had a very WASPy, buttoned-down way of expressing his feelings. (As evidenced by the title of his legendary comedy album *Button-Down Mind of Bob Newhart*.) A slight hesitation in his delivery would convey that he was troubled, and by slightly raising his voice he could express abject panic and fear.

Part of the way you achieve this moment-to-moment emotional clarity is through your writing. Remember that every setup should be clear about its subject *and* about your attitude toward it. Your punchlines should also be grounded in clear emotions.

To clarify what I mean by emotional fullness, let's take a look at an excerpt from Louis C.K.'s piece on playing board games with his kids (this excerpt precedes the "Monopoly" material we looked at in chapter 7). I'll indicate in parentheses the feelings that underlie his setups and punches.

Setup and punchline 1: (Annoyed) It's boring having kids. You have to play kid games. You have to play board games. Little kid board games where you go . . . (making the *monotonous* sound of a game spinner twirling). And you go tick, tick, tick.
Punchline 2: (Making the same *monotonous* sound again.)

Punchline 3: (Trying to hide his *frustration* from his daughter) You got a six, honey.

Punchline 4: (Acting out his daughter's *slow and methodical* counting and moving of her game piece) One . . . . Two . . . . Three . . . . . .

Punchline 5: (Openly *frustrated,* he points to where his daughter's game piece should go) It's here. Just go here. It's just . . .

Setup: (Acting out his daughter *standing up for herself*) Daddy, I'm learning.

Punch 1: (*Fed up*) I know, you're going to grow up stupid, 'cause I'm bored.

Punch 2: (*Fed up*) I can't take it baby, I can't.

Punch 3: (*Fed up*) I can't watch it.

Punch 4: (*Brutally frank*) I'm bored more than I love you.

Punch 5: (*Frank*) I can't. I just . . .

Every word in his jokes is grounded in a clear emotion. Your words should be too. You should be able to easily define that emotion; it should be obvious whether you're fed up, bored, excited, annoyed, afraid, ecstatic, etc. If you can't define the emotion, you need to rethink the joke. Adjust the writing so that it expresses how you feel about your subject.

The emotion should be as large as you can make it within your persona. Make a mountain out of everything. Hating something is funnier than being a little annoyed with it. Adoring something is funnier than liking it. Would you be more compelled to listen to a performer who said, "Here's something I'm a little annoyed about," or a performer who said, "Something happened to me and if it happens again I'm going to shoot myself"? A big part of what makes the Louis C.K. excerpt so funny is that he totally loses it with his little daughter although she hasn't done anything wrong or misbehaved. She's just being careful and taking her time. He's not paternally amused or annoyed by her. He can't stand it. She's driving him crazy. He can't take it anymore. If it doesn't stop he's going to lose his mind.

Part of your job as a stand-up is to so dominate the room with your presence that the audience can't help but give all their attention to you. Building a strong emotional life into your writing is a big part of accomplishing this.

The other big part, of course, is how you go about performing these emotions.

Essentially, there have been two schools of thought about how actors should act. One school contends that in order to successfully perform an emotion, the performer needs to actually feel it. The other contends that the actor needs to perform the *form* of the emotion, whether or not he's feeling it. Both of these approaches turn out wonderful actors. But within the world of theater, a fierce debate rages as to which of these approaches is the superior.

In the world of stand-up, however, there is no debate. A stand-up always performs the form of the emotion, not the real emotion. The reason for this is simple: in order to laugh, the audience must know the stand-up is all right. We can't worry and laugh at the same time. If we thought Lewis Black was really having a nervous breakdown we wouldn't sit there and laugh at him; we'd call 911. If we saw someone really angry about something, our first instinct would be to get away from him. The last thing we'd want to do would be to pull up a chair, order a drink, and laugh at him. Yet this is exactly what we do when a stand-up goes on a rant. Comedians give us the license to laugh at their pain by always providing us with a glimpse of the skin between their face and their comic mask. We know that the comedian is not really upset or fed up or pissed off. We know that we're witnessing the comic form of his or her emotions, and not the real emotions. The comedian is in control and doing fine.

Earlier in the book, I addressed your apprehension about considering yourself to be a comedy writer. I pointed out that when you said funny things, you were in fact, writing; writing with your mouth. Now let's address acting.

You already know how to act. You do it all the time. When you get tough with someone or flirt or pretend you're surprised when you aren't or pretend that you love something you don't love ("Oh my God! This is just what I wanted!! An ashtray with 'I love you' written on it!") or pretend that you're fascinated by someone who is boring you, you are acting. Furthermore, you are doing the kind of acting a stand-up does. You aren't really feeling it. You are acting the form of the feeling.

So, Mr. or Ms. Funny Person, just as you are a writer by virtue of being funny, you are an actor by virtue of being alive.

For a stand-up, there is one simple key to acting: know what attitudes you're playing and act them out. Know, for instance, that when you're doing a joke about how you fell in love today and your setup line is "You will not believe what happened to me today!"—that your attitude is delighted. It's not fed up or annoyed, it's delighted.

Some new stand-ups don't realize that performing stand-up is acting. So they don't think through and define the emotional life that underpins their jokes. They think that professional stand-ups just go onstage and talk, and that whatever emotions they express are coming out of them spontaneously.

It's no accident that so many stand-ups go on to enjoy successful acting careers. Through performing their stand-up, they've become such good actors that people in a comedy club, seated just a few feet away from them, don't realize that what they're saying is material that's been written and rehearsed. Often, these people are shocked if they see the stand-up in another performance and he is saying the same things in the same way.

Knowing the words of your jokes doesn't mean you're prepared to perform stand-up. You're prepared when you know both the words and the emotions that underpin them.

By being emotionally full onstage, you come alive to your audience. You achieve emotional fullness by building strong and clear attitudes into your writing and acting them out in performance.

28

BE IN THE ROOM

FOR A COMEDY CLUB AUDIENCE to give its full attention to a stand-up, they need to feel that he or she is talking not *at* them or even *to* them but *with* them, as if they are in a conversation with the stand-up. The stand-up's part of the conversation is his or her words. The audience's part of the conversation is their laughter and applause. They need to feel that they and the stand-up are in the room together sharing an experience.

There's a convention in the theater called the *imaginary fourth wall*. What this means is that if you were in a theater watching a scene taking place, say, in the living room of an English country home in the time of Queen Victoria, one wall might have a picture window overlooking a garden. Another wall might have a painting of an ancestor and the door to the library. The third wall might have the front door. And the fourth wall, the one that would be blocking the audience's view if it were actually there, is imaginary—but the actors pretend it's there. So if Lady Gwendolyn is telling Lord Marlborough that she thinks their son is sleeping with the upstairs maid and she fears a terrible scandal, and then someone in the audience sneezes loudly, Lady Gwendolyn isn't going to look out into the audience and say, "Gesundheit." She's going to pretend that she didn't hear that sneeze, even though everyone knows she did. And no one in the audience will feel Lady Gwendolyn is being impolite to the gentleman in the audience who just sneezed, because everyone understands she is in one place and time—her living room during the reign of Queen Victoria—and the audience is in another place and time: the theater in the present.

There is no imaginary fourth wall in a comedy club. Everybody is in the same room at the same time. As a stand-up, you can't pretend the audience is not there. You need to "be in the room" with them. So if you're onstage and someone in the audience sneezes loudly, you can, if you wish, and if it doesn't interrupt the flow of your joke, say "God bless you." If the person sneezes really loudly and you say "God bless you" really loudly, you'll probably get a laugh.

That is another reason to be in the room—you'll get more laughs. It is virtually a surefire laugh to acknowledge something unplanned and noticed by the whole room. One of the most famous examples of this technique came not from a stand-up, but from a president—John F. Kennedy. By employing it, he successfully handled what could have been an embarrassing moment at a dinner in Houston honoring a congressional ally. He was talking about the imminent launch of what at the time would be the largest missile sent into space. Kennedy meant to say that the US would be taking the lead against Russia in the space race by firing the biggest *payload* into space. But he misspoke. He said the US was about to fire the biggest *payroll* into space. This slip of the tongue caused a deadly silence in the room. Kennedy could have just corrected himself and moved on with his prepared remarks. But he had too keen a sense of humor to do that. He did correct himself, but then he paused, smiled, and said, "It will be the largest payroll, too." He got a huge laugh and sustained applause. This moment is often referenced to as one of the best examples of Kennedy's quick wit. And yet he didn't say anything witty. He got the laugh by acknowledging what everyone just heard. President Kennedy was in the room.

This simple technique is one of several you can employ to get additional laughs just by being in the room. The earlier chapters on crowd work and hecklers provide two additional techniques to make it clear to the audience that you are sharing the same time and space.

A fourth technique helps you handle a situation in which some people in the audience are not heckling you but have become too rowdy. If they're disturbing only you, it's best to just keep performing your act. For example, if the couple seated at the table right in front of you has, unfortunately for you, just come to the earthshaking realization that they're in love, and they are silently holding hands and staring deeply into each other's eyes and paying not one whit of attention to you—just keep going. If their inattention is bothering you, don't look at them and continue on with your set. No one but you knows this is going on, so no one but you is bothered. If you interrupt your set to chastise people who are innocent of any wrongdoing in the audience's eyes, the audience will feel that you are being unnecessarily hostile, and your likability will suffer.

On the other hand, if there are people at a table who are talking among themselves and disturbing both you and the audience, be in the room and make friends with them. Then ask them nicely and with humor to keep quiet. For example:

STAND-UP: (Addressing someone at the noisy table) Hey, my friend, where are you from?

NOISY GUY: Brooklyn.

STAND-UP: Brooklyn is in the house! What a great place. I love Brooklyn. You know, I think they can hear you in Brooklyn. If you could just keep it down to this area code that would be awesome. Deal? (Offers a fist bump.)

FORMER NOISY GUY: (Returning the fist bump) Deal.

You've made a friend and now your friend and his tablemates will be with you. You're their buddy.

The techniques I've described for you so far involve setting aside your planned set and either ad-libbing or, in the case of handling a heckler or doing written crowd work, appearing to ad-lib. But these aren't the only ways to be in the room. You can also accomplish this while sticking to your text by:

- Making eye contact with people. It's important for them to know you see them. If the stage lights are so bright that you can't actually see them, fake it. You know where they are.
- Holding for your laughs—that is, not talking at the height of their laughter—so they know you hear them as well as see them.
- Responding warmly to the audience when they give you applause at the beginning and end of your set. By doing this, you let them know that you are not only seeing them and hearing them but also feeling their appreciation.

People in the audience pay full attention to you when they feel *you* are paying full attention to *them*—when they feel that you are not up there delivering a speech to them, but rather are convivially conversing with them. Being in the room with them will open up additional opportunities to get laughs and help you maintain control over your audience.

29

DELIVERY

Two PEOPLE CAN SAY the same joke word for word, and one will get a laugh and the other won't. The difference is in their delivery. The factors that constitute delivery are pacing, timing, emphasis, and pauses. Let's look at each individually.

Pacing

Pacing refers to the overall speed of your delivery— you either talk fast or slow or in between. For a stand-up, the optimum pace is slow. Slow is funny. Underline that last sentence please. Going slow while maintaining strong energy is one of several performance skills that separate the pros from the wannabes. It's a technique that has been handed down from one generation to the next: Johnny Carson learned it from Jack Benny. Don Rickles learned it from his acting teacher, Sanford Meisner. Ellen DeGeneres learned it from Phyllis Diller. Bill Hicks learned it from Woody Allen who learned it from Bob Hope who learned it from an old, now-forgotten comedian who early in Hope's career pulled the young comedian aside backstage in a Texas vaudeville theater and told him that he wasn't getting big laughs because he was speaking so fast that the audience was having a tough time understanding him. He needed to slow down.

When you speed through your jokes, you don't have time to emotionally color them. When an audience is unable to see how you feel about what you're saying, you lack personality. You have no more personality than the voice in a drug commercial racing through the side effects. Also, when your pacing is fast the audience misses words, and even a single missed word can cost you a laugh. Another problem with speeding through your jokes is that you stop your audience from laughing long and hard. They can't because they don't want to miss what you're saying next.

Going fast sends an unintended message to your audience: *I don't want to take up your time. I know you're not all that interested in me, so I'll get this over with fast.* I remember one student of mine who was the fastest talker onstage I had ever encountered. When I asked him why he spoke so fast, he told me he was the MC at a strip club, and he knew the audience wasn't there to see him. I told him, "You need to make a big adjustment. From now on, don't think of yourself as the MC at the strip club. Think of yourself as the stripper. Take your time. Give them time to enjoy you. After all, they are there to see you."

Some people who speak too fast onstage but not offstage have an easy time slowing up. Essentially, all they need to do is remind themselves to slow down before they get onstage. Speaking at a normal speed is their default position, and a simple reminder puts them back on track. However, there are people who talk too fast both on- and offstage. They have a tougher time making this adjustment, because talking fast has become a habit for them; to their ears, it sounds normal.

For people who talk too fast all the time, they need to learn to slow down all the time, onstage and off. Here is one way to accomplish this: Pick two people who see you most every day. Tell them you're trying to slow down your speech and ask them to stop you if they hear you talking too fast. Having these people monitor your speech every day will help you slow down. Keep in mind that your ear is accustomed to your fast talking, so when you slow it down it will, at first, sound strange and unnatural to you. To the people you're speaking with, however, it will sound normal, and in time it will also sound normal to you.

Making this adjustment, you will reap benefits both on- and off-stage. Speaking slowly sends the message *What I have to say is worth hearing.* It sends this message of self-confidence quietly and forcefully. It contributes to making you a compelling communicator in all settings. In a comedy club, it will help establish you as a stand-up with a professional delivery.

Timing

Whereas pacing is the overall speed of your delivery, timing is the specific speed you employ in delivering the words and phrases that constitute a specific joke. Timing is altered to fit the needs of individual jokes. A stand-up who never altered her timing would come across to the audience as robotic and boring.

The key to effective timing is knowing the specific attitudes that underpin each of your jokes. Let's take as an example the famous Henny Youngman joke:

Setup: Women have really changed today. Take my wife . . .
Punchline: . . . please.

Say that setup out loud with the attitude *impressed.*
Now say it with the attitude *disgusted.*
Now say it *lovingly.*
Your attitude affects the way you time the line. You might deliver the line slower when you're impressed, faster when you're disgusted, and slower again when you're saying it with love. Knowing your attitude will guide you naturally to an effective timing of a line.

Emphasis

The third factor in delivery is emphasis: the words you vocally stress. In the chapter on setup and punchline, I passed along to you your comedy ancestors' instruction to vocally punch your punchlines.

To put a finer point on this invaluable piece of advice, there is always one specific word in the punchline that triggers the laugh—the punchword. Frequently the punchword is obvious: it's the last word in the joke. But there are times when this isn't the case and the obvious choice may be the wrong one.

For example, let's look at a line from the Rodgers and Hammerstein musical *Carousel.* It's spoken by a character named Jigger, a ruffian and petty thief. He's not the brightest of men. So, in a conversation about having babies, he delivers this laugh line:

My mother had a baby once.

Which word is the punchword? If your choice is *once*, you've chosen the wrong word. There's nothing particularly funny about being an only child. *My* is also the wrong choice; it implies that Jigger's mother, as opposed to other people's mothers, had a baby once, which doesn't make any sense.

The correct choice is *mother*. The line gets a laugh when it gets this delivery:

My *mother* had a baby once.

It's funny to see that Jigger thinks he's contributing to the conversation by pointing out that he knows someone who had a baby—his mother.

The punchword in a joke must be accurately identified and vocally emphasized for the audience to get the joke and laugh.

There is also a key word in the setup that needs to be stressed. It's the word that is most essential for the audience to hear and remember in order to get the punchline. For example, let's have another look at the Dangerfield joke about his promiscuous wife:

I got in a cab and told the driver, "Hey! Take me where the action is." He took me home!

The key word in the setup is *action*. The audience needs to know that's where Rodney wants to go—the place where the action is. The surprise in the punch is that the cabdriver knows where that place is—Rodney's home.

Identifying the punchword and the setup's key word will help guide you to the right emphasis for your delivery.

Pausing

There are two places in every joke where a pause is necessary. The first is **before the audience starts laughing**. After you've delivered your punchline, if you don't briefly pause, you'll step on your laugh; the moment you start talking again is the moment they stop laughing, and you don't want that moment to be right after you've delivered a punchline. This first pause should be very brief—not a *doctor's-office-deep-breath* inhale but a normal *I'm-starting-a-new-sentence* inhale.

It should last . . . that long.

In other words, it should last just long enough to give the audience the opportunity to laugh without worrying that they're going to miss what you're going to say next. On the other hand, it shouldn't last so long that it becomes obvious that you're waiting for them to laugh before you start your next joke.

It shouldn't last . . . . that long.

If the audience doesn't laugh but the stand-up takes a long pause, it becomes clear to everyone that the joke just bombed. If, however, your punch doesn't get a laugh but your pause is brief and you move swiftly on to your next joke, the audience is far less likely to realize that anything has gone awry. By moving on after a *new-sentence* inhale, you disguise the fact that you expected a laugh that you didn't get.

The second place where a pause is necessary comes **after the audience starts laughing**. This pause is called a *hold*.

You don't want to talk while the audience is laughing, for several reasons. First, they won't hear what you're saying. People can't hear you while they're laughing. Second, if they see that you're speaking while they are laughing, they'll stop laughing prematurely so they don't miss the next joke. You don't want to stop them from laughing—that's what they came to the club to do. The louder and longer they laugh, the more you'll have succeeded. Third, if you keep talking while they're laughing, it appears to the audience that you're not in the room, that you're delivering a prepared speech and it doesn't matter to you whether they laugh or not. That sense of your act being a spontaneous conversation with the audience is gone. The fourth reason is that when you don't hold for a laugh, you may be missing out on another possible laugh. Your hold itself can get a laugh. Let me explain.

A hold is made up of two parts. The first is listening. You need to listen to the audience's laughter. The volume of a laugh goes through three phases. In the first phase, right after your punch, the volume goes up as high as it's going to go. Sometimes that happens immediately; sometimes it takes a moment to build to that high point. In the second phase, the volume plateaus. In the third phase, the volume decreases until the laugh is gone. You don't want to be talking during phases one and two. You want to come back in at the very end of phase three, just before the laughter dies out completely. Letting it die completely before you come back in lets the energy seep out of the room. So the first part of getting good at a hold is getting good at listening to your audience.

What do you do while you're holding? You keep performing, without saying anything. This is the second part of a hold. It's the part where that additional laugh I was telling you about earlier can be achieved. During the hold, you want to silently keep performing the attitude that underpins your punch. So, let's say you're doing a joke about how your spouse can't cook, and your punch is "She put mayonnaise on my pastrami!" Your attitude on the punch is *Can you believe this?!* During the hold, through your facial expression and body language, you continue to communicate, *This is unbelievable, right?!*

The grand master of the hold was Jack Benny. As a comic flaw comedian, Benny himself was most often the target of his jokes and sketches. He often would stand with his arms folded across his chest. When a punchline that insulted him was delivered, he would raise the finger of one hand, delicately touch his cheek with it, and stare off into the distance with a look that expressed, *Good God, what I have to put up with.* Benny's hold always got a huge laugh. His hold was an "A+" laugh.

A stand-up who masters the hold can find places in his routine where he can get one laugh on his punch and a second on his hold.

There's another important benefit to holding for a laugh. It keeps you connected with your audience. Sometimes new comedians will use the time the audience laughs to think about their next line. Their mind is on the future. Sometimes they use this time to consider how their last joke was received. Their mind is in the past. In either case, it's clear to the audience that the stand-up is not with them in the present. In the present, they are laughing and the stand-up is not paying attention to them. The connection is momentarily broken.

But when a stand-up holds for a laugh and shares this moment with the audience by silently expressing to them how he feels about what he just said, the bond between the audience and the stand-up remains seamlessly connected. The audience feels, *I like this guy. He's here with us.*

So here is the sequence:

[End of punchline] He took me home!
Slight pause.
Laughter begins.
Hold.

There are many other ways a pause can heighten a joke. A pause can build tension, create suspense, express confusion or astonishment, to name just a few. Working out the delivery of your jokes in performance will guide you to where a pause will contribute to getting the biggest possible laugh. But the brief pause after you've delivered your punch, and the hold while the audience is laughing, must be part of every joke's delivery.

Your awareness of pacing, timing, emphasized words, and where you pause will lead you to a delivery that appears spontaneous to your audience and scores the maximum number of laughs, night after night after night.

30

THE THINGS TO DO BEFORE YOU GET TO THE CLUB

BEFORE YOU GET TO THE CLUB, there are some things you need to do to help ensure that your performance runs smoothly. Here is your *Before I get to the club* to-do list:

Time Your Set

Find out from the person producing the show how much time they want you to do. Then select material that lasts that long—actually, a little less, to make time for audience laughter and applause. So, for instance, if you're preparing a five-minute set, when you time yourself at home you should come in around four and a half minutes. That leaves 30 seconds for the audience's part of the proceedings.

It is of the utmost importance that you learn how to put together a set that brings you in on time. The only occasions when I've seen a club manager tell a stand-up never to return to the club is when that stand-up blew past his allotted time, ignored the club's stop signals (usually a flashing red stage light), and egregiously went over time. This is a cardinal sin in the world of comedy clubs. Here's the reason: Every club has a master schedule. Based on that schedule, club managers know when their staff needs to arrive and depart and what to tell patrons who ask what time the show starts and what time it ends. A "mic hog" puts all of this planning in jeopardy. He also puts his fellow performers in jeopardy, because the only way to stay on schedule when someone has blown way past his time is to cut out one of the remaining stand-ups.

If you're performing in a showcase with many stand-ups on the bill and you do less time than you've been allotted, that's OK. The stand-ups who perform after you can, if necessary, add some time to their sets. If, however, you're performing in a traditional comedy club show where you're one of only three stand-ups on the bill, doing less than your time creates problems. The club's patrons are expecting the show to run a certain amount of time, and if it runs noticeably shorter they feel cheated. One of my students landed a club gig to feature. (That's the middle spot between the opener and the head-liner.) The club asked her to do 30 minutes. She did 21. She never worked there again.

Coming in on time is the hallmark of a pro. It communicates to talent bookers that you know what you're doing. There's a story that Lorne Michaels, the longtime producer of *Saturday Night Live*, tells about casting the show's original company. Someone suggested that he see a young comedian named Chevy Chase. Michaels arranged for Chase to get stage time at a New York comedy club, and asked Chase to perform seven minutes there. Michaels describes Chase's performance as comic mayhem involving pratfalls and a slew of other physical-comedy "mishaps." Chase finished his performance; Michaels looked at his watch. Chase was in at exactly seven minutes. The "may-hem" had been timed down to the second. This made an indelible impression on Lorne Michaels and contributed to Chase getting cast.

Memorize Your Set

The way to memorize your set is to repeat it over and over again. This will hardwire it into your brain, so that it's there for you when you need it. Here are ways to memorize:

- Write the set down over and over again. Compare what you've written with your original text to see if you've made mistakes.
- Recite the set silently to yourself over and over again.
- Also recite the set out loud. If someone is willing to help you, have them read your set as they listen to you perform it. Ask them to make note of any mistakes. If you're working alone, voice-record yourself. With your set in hand, play back the recording to see where you're on target and where off target. Saying the set out loud will also help you hone your delivery.

OK, I'll do this, you may be thinking, *but what happens during my show if I forget something?* Have I already told you that you ask good questions?

Have Your Set on You

When you perform, you should always have a copy of your set on you, tucked away somewhere. When you become a star, performing your stand-up on television, your set will be written on offstage cue cards or monitors so that you can refer to them if you need to. Until then, have your set on you. If you know that all you need to remember each joke is a short cue of a word or two, you can write the whole set list on a slip of paper, ordering your cue words in the sequence you plan to use at the club. A set list can look something like this:

Candy Land
Monopoly
Take Me Home
Please
Diet
Blind Date
Shower
Reunion

If you're unsure how good your memory is—if you think you could look at a list like the one above and all that would come to your mind is *What the f—!* then write the whole set out, word for word. Plan on wearing something where you can tuck it away, and if you draw a complete blank onstage, take it out and use it. Don't go onstage holding it in your hand. You don't want to refer to it unless you absolutely must.

Some people write their sets on their hands and arms and try to sneak a look at them so the audience doesn't notice. Alas, the audience always notices. The best way to handle a memory freeze is to be in the room and, with humor, tell the audience what's happening. For example:

> Oh, this next thing I want to tell you about, it's hysterical. I love it. (Taking out notes) I love it but I can't remember it. (Reading notes) Oh yeah. . . .
> (Putting away notes and proceeding with the joke.)

Saying something like that is a virtually guaranteed laugh-and-applause break. You're in the room, you're saying something funny that appears to be spontaneous—it's an "A" laugh.

Select What You're Going to Wear

Our first impressions of people are based on how they look. Use this to your advantage. Pick out clothes that will help the audience see you the way you want to be seen. But also keep in mind the old show business rule of thumb that you want to be at least as dressed up as your audience is. You can be *more* dressed up than they are, but not less. People are paying money to see you. Out of respect for them, you don't want to wear clothes that are out of place for the occasion. For instance, when Rosanne Barr, the self-proclaimed "domestic goddess," made her *Tonight Show* debut, it was immediately clear from her appearance that this wasn't your usual hip, urban stand-up. As soon as she started talking, we could tell from her crass accent and too-loud voice that she came from the wrong side of the tracks. Just to be sure that we got the point, throughout her set she chewed gum. (Brilliant!) But she didn't wear an *it's-laundry-day-at-the-trailer-park* outfit. It was her *Tonight Show* debut. So she dressed the way a "domestic goddess" would dress for a special occasion: she wore an unfashionable print jacket and sported a large corsage. She looked like she was dressed to celebrate her anniversary at her local In-N-Out Burger. What she chose to wear that night vividly conveyed her persona, in a way that acknowledged the importance of her television debut.

An important part of establishing a comic persona is finding the right look. David Baker, for instance, a former student of mine from England, developed the persona of a clueless Brit living in the US. He'd wear either a suit and tie or a sport coat and dress shirt. Wearing these outfits, David consistently scored with audiences. (He went on to appear on *The Tonight Show*.) One night, as an experiment, he wore more casual clothes—casual pants and shirt, no jacket. It didn't work. His "A" jokes got a tepid response. The more formal look made it clear to the audience that David was a proper Englishman at sea in the USA. The more casual look undermined the clarity of his persona.

What you wear will help your audience see you the way you want to be seen. But you don't want them focused on your outfit, or your body either. Their attention should be on you and your comedy. Plunging necklines for women, open shirts for men . . . no. You want them to be in the moment with you, not fantasizing about some future private moment with you. It's also not a good idea to wear clothes with writing or pictures on them. The first thing the audience will do is fix their attention on your shirt. I saw a new stand-up who came onstage wearing a T-shirt with a great photo of David Bowie on it. I remember thinking, *That's probably the best picture of David Bowie that I've ever seen. And it's on a T-shirt. How is that possible? It's probably been through the wash a few times and yet it still looks like a museum-quality photograph. I wonder . . .* The next thing I knew, the stand-up was saying goodnight; I hadn't heard a word he said. But I still remember that T-shirt.

So don't wear clothing that will pull attention away from your jokes. You don't want their takeaway to be your outfit or body.

You have your set down to the required time, you have it memorized, you have your set on you, and you've chosen your outfit. Let's go to the club!

31

BEFORE THE SHOW STARTS

JUST AS THERE ARE THINGS you need to prepare before you get to the club, there are things you should—and shouldn't—do once you're there but before the show begins.

No Drugs or Alcohol

Do not drink alcohol or do recreational drugs before you get onstage. When you perform stand-up, your workplace, essentially, is a bar. It's a place that encourages its patrons to drink. You are not a patron; you are a performer. Don't get this confused. The thought that a drink will relax you before you perform makes as much sense for a stand-up as it does for an athlete. Can you imagine a tennis player at the US Open taking a drink to relax before a match? You, like that player, want to be at the absolute top of your game. Alcohol won't take you there—it will inhibit you from getting there. Just as a coach would be alarmed to see one of his players drinking alcohol before a game, a comedy show producer doesn't want to see a stand-up knocking them back at the bar before a show. A club usually puts out a pitcher of water for the performers. Take the hint.

Remember that it's normal to get nervous before a show. Your nerves won't hurt you, they will help you. The last thing you want to do is dull them with drugs or alcohol. If you find yourself getting nervous before a show, breathe. Sometimes when people get nervous their breathing becomes shallow; sometimes, people actually stop breathing. Alcohol, bad. Drugs, bad. Water, good. Oxygen, good. Take some deep breaths and a glass of water. They will give you a sense of well-being.

Mic Check

If you can check the mic before the show, get to the club early and do it. In a comedy club, the manager sets the volume of the microphone before the show starts and then moves on to other tasks. During the show, usually there is no one in the sound booth to adjust the volume of the mic. You don't want to overproject or underproject. Checking the volume of the mic before the audience is seated will let you determine how loud you should speak.

The Signal Light

The signal light signals you to either wrap it up or stop. Make sure you know where it is. If you don't, have someone point it out to you. Also, be certain of what the signal means. In some clubs, a blinking red light means it's time to wrap things up. Then, if you're taking too much time wrapping up, the light will stop blinking and become a solid red light, which means it's time to stop. When stand-ups get the blinking wrap-it-up light they will often signal the timekeeper that they've seen it by saying something like, "There's one last thing I want to share with you . . ." But some show producers don't give a warning light, so when the light goes on it means you've gone over your time and should stop immediately. So there's no confusion in your mind about what the light means, ask the club manager or show producer before you go onstage.

The Rundown

You need to know your spot in the rundown (the order in which the show's stand-ups perform). Once you get it, don't complain about it. Some new stand-ups believe that going first is bad, because the audience hasn't had much to drink yet. Others don't want to go toward the end of the rundown; they think their audience will be too focused on settling the tab to pay attention to them. Be assured of this: funny is funny whether you go at the beginning, in the middle, or at the end of the show. This comedy truth became clear to a group of my students when I took them to a stand-up show that was being broadcast live from a comedy club. The stand-up who killed it was the warmup act. If going first is a lousy spot, he should have been dead on arrival. Consider what he was up against: He performed before the televised show actually started. People were still getting seated. The first drinks hadn't made it to the table. The waitstaff was still taking first-round orders. None of the audience was there to see him; they were there to see the featured stand-ups. And yet none of the featured stand-ups came close to getting the response he did. After the show, the buzz was about him. Find out where you are in the rundown and then set your mind on killing it.

Your Introduction

If you have a name that might be mispronounced, let the MC know its proper pronunciation. Getting the performers' names right is an important part of the host's job. He'll be grateful for your help. If you've performed stand-up in the past and/or have future appearances lined up, it's good to have him mention it in your introduction; he'll be happy to do so. It is best not to give the MC something funny to say about you. It rarely gets laughs. Most important, when it's your stage time, the first laugh should come from you, not the MC.

Get into the Zone

When your preshow tasks are completed and you're waiting for the show to begin, it's time to "get into the zone." You may have arrived at the club in a good or bad mood. You may be really feeling up for performing, or like you'd rather have a root canal. The important thing to remember no matter how you are feeling is this: it doesn't matter how you feel. What matters is that you give a solid performance. That's a big part of being a professional stand-up (or a professional anything). When people pay you for your services, they expect you to do a good job. If you do a great job, that's terrific. But anything less than good is unacceptable. So no matter what your mood is when you get to the club, you need to get into the zone by the time the show starts.

The zone is a headspace that enables you to do your best performance. It's a mindset that ensures you will deliver your lines as you planned, with the attitudes that you've chosen to make your jokes work. You don't want the emotional life required by your jokes to be overwhelmed by feelings that have nothing to do with the jokes but everything to do with what happened to you that day. If, for instance, you were driving to the show and stopped at a red light, and the second the light turned green the guy behind you started honking his horn and cursing you out for being a lousy driver, you'll probably arrive at the club feeling angry. If you allow yourself to dwell on that thought until showtime, you'll bring that anger onstage with you. Or if it's your birthday and you just got a sweet text from your ex and are thinking how much you miss him or her, you'll arrive onstage feeling sad. If you bring feelings like these onstage, they'll color your delivery in ways that hurt the jokes. For example, if Henny Youngman delivered his "Take my wife—please" with anger or sadness, it would kill the laugh. Your mind needs to be in a good place where you can focus on performing your set as you've planned.

The first step toward getting to this good place is determining what environment puts you in a good frame of mind before the show starts. Some stand-ups enjoy the company of colleagues and friends before they go onstage. Others prefer to be by themselves in a quiet spot. Do whatever works for you.

The second step that takes you to the zone involves consciously selecting what you want to think about before you go onstage. Remember, to a great extent, how you feel is based on what you are thinking. You will find your way into the zone by replacing your preshow thoughts with this thought: *I'm going to have a great time talking to these people. I'm going to have a great time expressing myself. I'm going to have fun!* Let this be your preshow mantra. When you do, something wonderful happens: Your performances become an emotional sanctuary for you. They become a place you can go to and find enjoyment no matter what's gone down during the day. Irving Berlin penned the lyric "There's no business like show business." The man knew what he was talking about.

Taken together, the preshow preparations outlined in this chapter will enable you to perform at your full capacity.

32

SHOWTIME

You've memorized your set, your mind is focused on having a great time with the folks out front, the MC is introducing you. It's time to give you some pointers on what to do next.

Timing Your Entrance

The timing to start your set is identical to the timing of a hold. You want to start speaking right at the tail end of the audience's applause. You don't want to start when it's at its loudest, because they'll have trouble hearing you. You don't want to wait until the applause is gone and the room is silent, because that lets the energy seep out of the room. There is an exception. If your intent is to build tension in the room rather than energy, a long pause after the applause is over will do the trick. Unless tension is what you want, start speaking at the tail end of the applause.

In order to accomplish this, you need to do something counterintuitive during the MC's introduction. The intuitive thing is to wait in the back of the club, listen to your introduction, and when it's over start toward the stage. If you time your entrance this way, you will arrive onstage too late. In addition to the time it takes walking to the stage, you also need time to adjust the microphone before you start talking. If you wait until your introduction is over before you start to the stage, you will run out of applause before you've accomplished these two tasks.

Here's the proper way to time your entrance: Between acts the MC either does a bit of stand-up and then introduces the next performer, or goes right into the next performer's intro. If the MC is doing some jokes, wait. When you hear that your introduction is starting, start walking toward the stage. Don't arrive onstage until the MC has finished your introduction. When he's finished, optimally, you want to be one or two steps away from the stage. This will enable you to arrive onstage at the height of the audience's applause, giving you adequate time to adjust the microphone and acknowledge the applause before you begin your set.

Adjusting the Microphone

The first thing to do when you get onstage is to adjust the microphone; you want to make sure the audience can hear you. There are two ways to use the mic. The first is to leave it in the microphone stand, and the second is to hold it in your hand. Both are equally good. Over time you want to get good at doing both. In either case, there is one place and only one place the microphone needs to be and that is right under your mouth and pointed toward you.

Club microphones are illusively designed. Because they're usually round, they look like they will amplify your voice no matter what part of it you speak into. But that's not the case, for good reason: There are peripheral noises going on during the show—people ordering and consuming food and drink, as well as the general murmur of the crowd. An omnidirectional microphone would pick up and amplify all of these sounds. So comedy clubs use unidirectional microphones that amplify only the performer's voice. There is no amplification if you speak into the sides of these microphones. So to be amplified, you need to speak into the top. Singers usually put the top of the mic right in front of their mouths. This gives them maximum amplification; however, it blocks their face. Stand-ups want the audience to see their face, so they hold the mic right under their mouth, tilted toward their mouth. This method ensures both that their face is clearly seen and that their voice is fully amplified. The next time you watch a professional stand-up, watch how he or she holds the mic and you'll see what I'm describing.

When you handhold the mic, put the stand behind you; don't leave it center stage. *You* should be center stage, not a metal pole. Also, if you don't put the stand behind you, it will block the view of the people seated directly in front of it.

When you finish your set, thank the audience, and while they're applauding, move the stand back to its center-stage position, put the microphone back in the stand, and wave good-bye. It's your responsibility, not the MC's, to return the microphone and stand to their proper place.

Starting Your Set

If inspiration strikes you on the way to the mic, strike it back with everything you've got. Start with your first prepared joke. You've chosen it because it's an "A" joke and gives the audience a picture of your personality. And because it's been tested, the odds are it will work. You have no idea how an untested spur-of-the-moment quip will be received, and the worst place for a joke to fail is right up front. This is the time the audience is making up their minds whether or not you're funny. The time to take chances with untested material, like the hilarious idea you just came up with on your way to the mic, is after you've already got the audience laughing. At that point, they've made up their minds that you're funny and it doesn't matter to them if a joke doesn't work—they are with you.

What to Do If a Joke Doesn't Work

The sooner you embrace the following concept, the sooner you'll get good at stand-up: If you have a good time when a joke works, your audience will have a good time. If you have a good time when a joke doesn't work, your audience will still have a good time. They feel what you feel, remember? People go to comedy clubs to have fun, not to evaluate each of the stand-ups' jokes. In all my years of producing shows, I've never heard an audience member after the show say, "I thought the redhead's first two jokes were good. I thought he missed badly on the third, but made a comeback on four and five." This is what I do hear: "That redhead was funny!" You do not live or die by the audience reaction to a joke; if an occasional one doesn't work, nothing is lost unless you get thrown by it. But if a minute or so of your material doesn't work, you're in trouble. I will tell you how to deal with this situation in a moment.

Having a perfect show is a lousy goal; no one cares and you shouldn't either. If perfection is your goal, comedy is not for you. Great stand-up comedy is not written, it is rewritten—and rewritten and rewritten for as long as it takes to make it work. So if you feel that you've failed when a new joke doesn't work, you will never write good stand-up material. You should strive to always do your best, not to be perfect. If you have the commitment to work on your jokes, delivery, and persona until you get undeniably good and give consistently strong performances, you have a future in this business. Forget about perfection. For a stand-up, the goal of perfection is the shortcut to failure.

So when a joke doesn't get a laugh, know that nothing has gone wrong, keep your composure, and do one of the following things: (1) Just keep going. A lot of times the audience doesn't know you've delivered a punchline, so they don't know anything went wrong. All is well. Move on to the next joke. (2) If another line related to the joke enters your head, say it. Sometimes you're only one sentence away from that joke getting a laugh. (3) If you sense that the audience clearly knows your joke has bombed, that's a setup for getting a laugh with a *save*.

A save is what you say or do to acknowledge that a joke didn't work. It's another way of being in the room. A save does not involve putting yourself down as a performer. If, after a joke doesn't work, you say something like, "I suck at this. Sorry," you will totally bum out the audience. If you start feeling bad, so will they. A save involves acknowledging that the joke didn't work. When Johnny Carson's studio audience didn't laugh at a joke, Johnny would stare right into the camera with an alarmed expression. He'd look like he was signaling those of us at home to call 911 because his studio audience was about to kill him. This save was a reliable "A+" laugh. It was an aspect of Johnny's genius that helped him create an indestructible opening monologue night after night. He got big laughs when his jokes worked. He got bigger laughs when they didn't work.

David Letterman also had a famous save. When he was at his desk doing jokes that involved something written on a card and the joke didn't work, he'd silently turn toward the set "window" behind him and throw the card into it. There would be the sound of breaking glass, followed by a thud. He'd get his "A+" laugh with this save and move on to his next joke.

Rock Albers always carried a megaphone onstage, which he'd put down on the floor next to him. When a joke bombed, he'd pick it up and repeat the punchline over the megaphone as if the problem was that we just didn't hear it. Big laugh.

Saves have to be used sparingly. If done too often, they bring attention to the fact that a lot of your jokes aren't working. Used sparingly, they enable you to get laughs on jokes that don't work.

Bombing

It's one thing to open your set to strong laughs and then have a joke or two not work. It's another thing to perform your opening "A" jokes to stony silence. But there are moves you can make to turn around this most dreaded of situations.

The first is to follow the example of Chris Rock. When he feels that he's not connecting with an audience, his first move is to slow down. A bad mistake often made by newbies is to speed up when the audience isn't laughing. If you do this, you might as well just throw in the towel. If they're not getting you, if they're not laughing, the reason may very well be that you're talking too fast and they can't clearly make out what you're saying or sense what you're feeling. So the first move is to slow down.

The second move is to change up your set list. As I'll explain in more detail later, the problem may be that the material you've selected is inappropriate for your audience. Maybe they're too young or too old, or too conservative or too rowdy, for the jokes you planned on performing. When your repertoire of jokes gets big enough, you can customize your set to fit a particular audience. Also, you can change up your set list while you're performing to better connect with your audience.

Those are the first two moves to make. If they don't get the audience laughing, it's time to make the third move.

If you continue performing your written material to an audience that isn't laughing, you become elevator music; you become background noise. Your audience starts to feel that the situation is OK with you. They start talking among themselves. You're talking, they're talking; everybody's talking and having a nice time. You can't let that happen. You have to take charge of the room. The way to do this is through crowd work. Start talking to individual people in the audience. They have to listen to you if you're directly talking to them. Ask them questions, engage them in conversation. If you have written crowd work with good punchlines, work that material into your conversation. Get those people laughing. Get their table laughing. And the next table. It's comedy hand-to-hand combat. It's the last resort, but it can save the day.

If all this fails to win over the audience and you totally bomb, consider this: Every comedian bombs. It happens. The only people who never bomb are people who never perform. Don't blame the audience; don't get angry at them or at yourself. Finish up and thank them. Afterward, work to figure out why you bombed. It will make you better prepared to handle future indifferent audiences. Bombing doesn't mean you've failed. It means you're engaged in the process of becoming a professional stand-up. Dust yourself off and get back on the stage as soon as you can.

Ending Your Set

When you've delivered your last joke, make eye contact with your audience and graciously thank them. This is an important moment. The warmer your thank-you, the bigger your applause. Always remember: the audience feels what you feel. If you end your set by giving your audience a perfunctory thank-you, and you fail to make eye contact with them because you're focused on putting your microphone back in place, they'll respond with a perfunctory round of applause.

Another surefire way to get an unenthusiastic farewell is to end your set with a stand-up cliché. At the time I'm writing this, the current open mic farewell is "That's my time." A regular audience doesn't know that stand-ups are given a limited amount of time to perform. If you end with that cliché, not only have you failed to thank the audience, they don't even know what you're talking about. It's a ridiculous way to end a set. Swear to me you won't end your set that way. I mean it. We've already come a long way together—don't let me down now!

A third way to leave the stage to the sound of flapping moth wings is to end your set with an apology like "That's all I have." Never apologize during your set. When you're performing stand-up, you are your own public relations firm. Don't put negative thoughts about your work into your audience's minds. Stand-ups who end their performance with that apology are inviting a friendly audience to suddenly question their work: "He was good, but that's all he's got. The others had more. Too bad."

No matter how you think your performance went, always finish strong with a warm and gracious thanks to your audience. It's a simple way to leave them with a positive impression of you.

Congratulations on your performance. Now, how do you get from well-grounded beginner to successful pro? Read on.

Part V

GET UNDENIABLY GOOD

33

BUILDING AN ALL "A" SET

IN ORDER TO START GETTING PAID AS A STAND-UP, you need a set that elicits an unbroken string of strong laughs from beginning to end, consistently, night after night. This is what I call an *all-"A" set.* Here's a simple way to understand the paramount importance of achieving this. If you have an all "A" 5-minute set, you'll get paid nothing. If you have a 10-minute all "A" set, you may get paid by a headliner to be one of his or her opening acts. Also, some big-city clubs have shows that showcase new professionals. These shows typically pay a performer around $35. If you have 20 minutes of "A" material, you can start getting booked at roadhouses. Roadhouses are clubs outside of major cities. They're where most pro stand-ups make their living. Typically, they book three comedians for a show. The stand-up who goes first is called the MC and opener; the one who goes in the middle is called the featured act; and the stand-up who is drawing the audience into the club is called the headliner and goes last. The typical pay for the opener is in the low three digits. The featured performer, who needs to have about 30 minutes of solid material, is usually paid in the high three digits to the low four digits. The headliner—who needs to have an hour of "A" material, television performing credits, and/or a very large social media following—can easily make 10 times what the featured act makes. And in big-city venues like Gotham Comedy Club in New

York, headliners can make between $40,000 and $70,000 to appear in shows over a weekend. The more you write, the more "A" jokes you'll come up with—and the more you'll get paid.

For this reason, I urge you to schedule time during the week to write. Don't make the schedule idealistic, make it realistic. Factor into it all of your other work and personal obligations. Make it doable and then do it. Don't get blown off it. Treat it the way you treat your other work-related responsibilities. Because bottom line, stand-up comedy is a business, and it's a business that you own. If you get good at it, people will start paying you to perform. As a business owner you must learn to think entrepreneurially. That means you must take your stand-up career as seriously as you take your other work endeavors. You must be prepared to intelligently invest the time, money, and energy needed to make it succeed. It's up to you—no one else can do this for you. And that's a wonderful thing. In other areas of the performing arts and entertainment industry a lot of people—directors, producers, agents, publishers, executives, to name a few—stand between you and your opportunity to have an audience experience your work.

When you make your writing schedule, take into account the environment in which you most enjoy writing. Some people enjoy writing in cafés. Others want a quiet place to write. A number of great writers, including Woody Allen and Stephen Sondheim, like to write in bed. Some writers like to write at a particular time of day or night. Some can write anywhere, anytime. Set yourself up to write in the places and at the times you most enjoy writing.

In addition to putting in the time to write, building an all "A" set requires several other things. First, you have to make up your mind that you will not settle for small laughs. I sometimes hear comics defend a weak joke by saying, "It gets a laugh." That's true. It gets *a* laugh. A laugh does not lead to *a* career. You headline when you rock the house from the beginning to the end of your set.

Second, you need to listen to your audience. To repeat, I'm not referring to an open mic audience consisting exclusively of other stand-ups waiting to perform. I'm referring to regular, paying audiences. Their response to your material will tell you where the strength in your act is, which areas need work, and which material you should toss. Your audience is your editor in chief.

For this reason, you should always audio record your club performances. An actual recording of your performance is a far more accurate means of capturing the audience's response to your jokes than your memory is. When you record, leave your device in the back of the club; don't bring it onstage with you. The primary thing you want to capture is the audience's laughter. Although an audio recording can help you evaluate some aspects of your performance—such as your timing, your inflections, and your volume—these considerations are secondary to this one: *How big was the laugh?* Evaluating yourself is more subjective than evaluating the audience's laughter. You can grade the volume and length of a laugh with a degree of objectivity that you don't have when you're trying to assess your own performance. If the laugh was big, you were performing the joke correctly.

Grading your laughs should take place well after you've left the stage; you don't want to be doing that while you're performing. Onstage, your sole focus should be having a great time with your audience.

The letter grades for laughs are "A," "B," and "C." An "A" laugh is the big laugh—everyone in the audience laughing loudly. A joke that gets an "A" laugh around 75 percent of the time, from audiences both generous and tough, is an "A" joke.

Jokes that sometimes get big laughs and sometimes get smaller laughs are "B" jokes. "C" jokes get chuckles or nothing at all. What you want to do with "B" and "C" jokes is move them up to "A's."

Here's how: The first move is to perform the joke several more times. This will give you more confidence in the delivery, which may be all the joke needs to move up to an "A." In the theater, if you see the first public performance of a play, it's not going to be nearly as good as seeing it after it's been running for a while. The words are the same. What's changed is the actors' more assured delivery.

If, after several performances of the joke, its grade doesn't go up, the second move is to clarify and shorten it. Make sure the setup has only one subject so that you're pointing the audience clearly in the direction of the punch. Make sure your attitude toward the subject is clear. See if you can restate the punchline in fewer words. The essence of punching up a joke is taking out all unnecessary words.

If those two steps don't bring up the joke's grade, then it's time to use my secret weapon. Please feel free *not* to pass along what I'm about to tell you. Hey, you paid for this book; if you want to withhold this information from the competition, remonstrations will certainly not come from me.

The final and ultimate way of moving a joke up to an "A" is to change the attitude underpinning the joke to its exact opposite. For example, let's look again at Laura Bassi's babysitting jokes from page 61. This was the first draft:

> I don't like babysitting infants. They don't do anything and you have to talk to them in a baby voice all day, like (in baby voice) "Aaawww who's the best baby, who's the best baby." And what's the point? They don't understand anything anyway . . . and they're completely unempathetic. Even when I complain and tell them that six more people got engaged on Facebook today. And that Justin and Leah bought a house and I'm living in a hallway. They just lie there.

But when Laura applied my secret weapon to these jokes, the piece transformed into this:

> My favorite age to babysit are infants, because they're amused by anything you say, as long as you use the right inflection. So I just use it as a therapy session. And I'll be like (in baby talk voice), "Hey! Six more people got engaged on Facebook today! (Makes her hand into a gun and shoots at her head) Pshew! And Justin and Leah bought a house! I live in . . . a hallway.

In performances, this rewrite of Laura's jokes consistently got "A" laughs. She achieved this by replacing the attitude *I don't like babysitting infants* with *My favorite age to babysit are infants*. If a joke has potential but needs a significant rewrite, the best way to start is by coming at it with an attitude that's the opposite of its original one.

In my experience, if you can get a "C" joke up to a "B," then with additional work you can get it up to an "A." But sometimes jokes don't budge, no matter how much work you put into them. Here's what you do with these recalcitrants: if it's a "B" that gets a solid laugh and you need a few of them to fill out your allotted time, keep it. But if it's stuck as a "C" joke after it's been tweaked and performed several times, then cut it. Chuckles don't get you anywhere. You lose your audience with chuckles.

Using this grading system, Laura wrote the successful final draft of her animal-noises piece (see page 118). In performance, the jokes about the real pig sounds never scored more than "C" laughs. So they were cut:

> Everyone tries to teach their kids animals sounds because it's cute, but half the sounds aren't even what the animals say . . . ~~Pigs say "OINK!" Pigs don't say OINK. Pigs say (makes real pig noise) That's not cute. No one wants their child walking around going, (makes pig noise twice).~~

Most of the lines about what men say got "B" laughs. The line that didn't was "Dang, girl, you look good. Come over here!" It was cut.

> Sometimes men are pigs, so what do pigs say? ~~"Dang girl you look good come over here!" (Whistles.)~~ "Hey I'm super drunk and not ready for a relationship. You wanna come over?"

Laura did two things to move those "B" laughs up to "A's." She realized that if she changed the subject, she could make the punch a total surprise. She also tweaked the wording of the punchline and added a second punch. Here's the final version of the material to this point:

> One thing parents love to teach their kid are animal sounds. But I don't get it. Because they teach them, "Pigs say oink," but pigs don't say "oink." Pigs say . . . "I'm a drunk twentysomething

male at a bar. Who's not ready for a relationship but doesn't want to be lonely."

Because this joke got a strong "A" laugh, she wrote a follow-up joke that also got an "A" laugh:

Cows say moo; nope, no they don't. Cows say, "Hi, I'm Laura Bassi and I just ate two thousand calories before this show!"

The final joke got a "B" laugh in performance. Laura was able to move it up to an "A" simply by tightening it:

I don't know why we don't teach them something useful for their life. Like "What does a twenty-seven-year-old who still babysits as a job say?" . . . "HELP!!" "Don't ever major in communications!"

This rewriting process enabled Laura to take a funny but rambling and uneven piece of comedy and transform it into all "A" jokes.

Earlier I stated that it's fine to have some "B" jokes in your set if you need them to fill out your time. But that applies only to regular gigs; there are other times when you need to do your absolute best. Industry showcases, contests, auditions for clubs, comedy festivals, and television, or a night when someone important in the industry is in the audience—occasions like these call for what stand-ups refer to as their *industry sets*. These sets are composed exclusively of not just "A" material but *original* "A" material. Some "A" jokes are generic, formula jokes—for instance, the "half-and-half" joke:

I'm half German and half Irish. I'm a very disciplined drunk.

Such jokes can get big laughs from an audience, but industry professionals have heard them before. So when it comes time to prepare my students for the American Comedy Institute Industry Showcase, I tell them to cut any "A" laughs that anyone could tell. I want what comes out of their mouths to be not only funny but also so stamped with their own unique personas that no other stand-up could possibly tell it as well.

Building and growing an original "A" set is a lifetime endeavor. There are solid "A" jokes that, because of their subjects, have a limited shelf life and will need at some point to be replaced with new material. A stand-up may have killer jokes about news events that quickly become dated and stop working; news tends to get old pretty fast. There are other kinds of jokes with clear expiration dates, such as jokes about aspects of a stand-up's changing personal life. If you were fat years ago but you've since lost the excess weight, the fat jokes will stop working. Audiences have to feel that you're talking about things that are red-hot issues for you right here and now. In comedy, the past is only funny when it still has you by the throat.

There are jokes, like those written by Mark Twain quoted earlier, that remain fresh and funny perhaps forever. But because of the ever-increasing array of new platforms for entertainment, stand-ups must constantly engage in writing new jokes. In the days of vaudeville, before radio and television, a comedian could hone a 20-minute act and perform it, unchanged, in theaters across the country for many years and never encounter an audience member who had heard it before. But advances in technology continually make it easier and cheaper to reach large groups of people. That in turn creates a need for comedians to have a steady stream of new material. Tig Notaro's joke about her breast cancer, recorded at a club, went viral and was seen by tens of thousands of people worldwide in a matter of days.

A good way to think about how to meet the demand for new material is to think of your writing as two pipelines. In the first pipeline are jokes that you're currently performing. You want to hone them until they become solid "A" jokes. Put in the work. Don't settle for tepid laughs. Even if a joke is getting solid laughs, see if you can find a way to make it better; rewrite it and try it out.

A good example of this is Tig Notaro's breast cancer joke. When she first performed it she did an act-out of her breasts "responding" to her constant criticism of them by saying,

You know what, we're sick of this. Let's leave.

That punchline got a good laugh, but Notaro wasn't satisfied with it. She saw a way to make the joke even stronger by raising the stakes:

You know what, we're sick of this. Let's kill her.

This process of rewriting jokes and then working, in performance, on finding the optimum way to deliver them is what goes on in the first pipeline.

In the second pipeline are brand-new jokes that haven't been performed yet. They haven't made it into the first pipeline yet. They are first drafts. Remember them? It's important not to forget the discipline of the first draft:

- Don't throw anything out until you try it out
- Be an easy grader at the outset of a joke's life

The biggest mistake you can make in a first draft is to throw out a joke prematurely. If you apply the same rigorous standards to a new joke that you apply to the jokes you're already using in performance, the chances increase that you'll throw out material that could become "A" material jokes. Don't forget that it took you time and effort to hone your tried-and-true material. It's a mistake to get too conservative. Trying out new jokes is a risk, but it's a risk you need to take in order to meet the demand for fresh material and stay vibrant and alive as a comedy artist.

The audience doesn't see all the work that goes into writing stand-up comedy. All they see is that you're incredibly funny in a way that's uniquely your own. The hard work is our secret.

The great comedian Groucho Marx said there are two things to look for to determine whether or not a comedian is going to make it. One is that the comedian knows how to edit his material. He knows what to keep and what to throw out. Now you know how to do that. The second thing Groucho said to look for is the subject of the next chapter.

34

CREATING YOUR PERSONA

GROUCHO'S SECOND CRITERION FOR DETERMINING whether or not a comedian will succeed is the clarity of his or her persona. This is the second key to getting good.

For a stand-up, the process of creating a persona is like sculpting a piece of wood: the carving is done with your hands and the hands of many audiences. Sculpting is about cutting things away; there is less wood at the end than there was in the beginning. The work of art is what's left. The same is true in creating a stand-up persona.

There are two questions to ask yourself when you're reviewing the recordings of your performances. The answers to these questions will help you create your persona. After you get a big laugh, ask yourself this question: *What was I talking about?* There are certain subjects that audiences will enjoy hearing you talk about more than others. Big laughs are invitations to write more about those subjects. The same question should be asked about jokes that tank. The absence of laughs can indicate the subjects that don't work for you. It can be a signal not to write jokes on that subject.

Let me give you an example. I had a student who had a comically hapless persona. He joined the navy and on the first day of basic training all the recruits were asked to dive into a pool. They did. After a few moments all their heads bobbed up from the water. All but his.

He didn't know how to swim. When the instructors realized he was missing, they jumped in the water and saved him. He almost drowned on the first day of his navy career. His audiences gave him big laughs on the jokes about his navy career and the jokes about his current job—managing a nuclear power plant. However, when he delivered jokes about his sex life . . . crickets. Even though these jokes were well written and carried forward the theme of his haplessness, for some reason, night after night, audiences didn't want to hear about his sex life. So he dropped the subject.

Learning which subjects work for you and, just as important, which ones don't, helps you to crystallize your persona.

The second question to ask yourself when a joke gets a big laugh is *What attitudes did I play on that joke?* The big laugh is an invitation to write more jokes where you can play those same attitudes. And as before, ask the same question when a joke is followed by the sound of lint falling on a T-shirt. The absence of a laugh can indicate that the joke's attitudes don't work for you.

Here's an example. Rock Albers was never funnier than when he played the attitude of anger. His fury was stoked by the oddest things, such as how states select their state birds, or the lack of diversity in the astrological signs of US congressmen. You might think these jokes would work if Rock played them with the attitude of sarcasm. But in our work together it became apparent that when a joke was under-pinned by sarcasm, it didn't work. He had to be sincerely enraged. Anger worked for him; sarcasm didn't. We wrote a lot more angry jokes.

By writing more jokes about the subjects and with the attitudes that work best for you, and by eliminating the subjects and attitudes that don't work, you will, over time, find your persona.

I've heard from some students who've taken other workshops that at the very outset of the course they were encouraged by their instructor to act out a persona based on their physical appearance and how they come across to their fellow students. That is a mistake.

I don't know of a single successful comedian whose persona is identical to his or her offstage personality. Sarah Silverman is not an airhead racist; Lewis Black is not constantly in the throes of a nervous breakdown; Gilbert Gottfried doesn't yell. And Steve Martin doesn't run around in a white suit with a tomahawk in his head. (This seemed to have come as a shock to some people who attended a live interview with Martin in New York. He spoke of his current interests and activities—his avid art collecting and finishing his latest novel. No tomahawk. A lot of people wanted their money back.)

A persona is not a stand-up's offstage personality. It may have some aspects of it. But ultimately it's a creation of the stand-up's imagination, produced in conjunction with audiences over a span of, usually, several years.

There's another reason not to jump prematurely into a persona, whether it's close to who you are or is clearly a made-up character. Once you lock in to a persona, everything you write and perform needs to be aligned with it. If you choose one prematurely, it will very likely lack the complexity and depth that will enable you to express all that you want to say with your comedy. It will be cartoonish. I had a talented student who began his career in my workshop. He was smart and funny. Shortly after leaving the workshop, he appeared in a show which I happened to see. He was wearing a straw hat and speaking in a hillbilly accent. His material reflected a backward hillbilly's point of view. There was no trace of the intelligent comedy he was capable of creating, and, just as important, this persona lacked authenticity. He came across as an actor in a sketch comedy show portraying a rural rube. The audience's response to his set was tepid. If audiences don't buy into your persona, you are, as they say in the hills of Kentucky, a goner. When I asked him about his choice of this persona, he told me that some people liked it and some people thought it was too much and that he should tone it down. In real life, people don't say things to you like, "You know, Steve, I think your personality is a little over the top. Take it down a few notches." Such things are also not said to a stand-up who has successfully created a persona.

The organic process of creating a persona can't usually be completed in a few weeks or months. Typically, it takes many performances and many audiences for a believable persona to come into being. Jumping into one, like jumping into a Halloween costume, entertains people for only a very short amount of time. "Oh you're a skeleton!" Now what?

There are ways to move this process along as quickly as possible. The first is to give yourself the freedom at the beginning of your career to talk about anything you want. The best way to find the subjects that work for you is to talk about whatever enters your comic mind. The second thing is to be emotionally full when you perform. The way to find the emotions that work best for you is to vividly perform a wide range of them.

35

THE SIX CHARACTERISTICS OF A SUCCESSFUL PERSONA

THERE ARE MANY GENERIC STAND-UPS. It's difficult to remember their names. They can be amusing, but they're never memorable. And then there are the stand-ups who pop out of the generic pack. They are unforgettable. There is no one quite like them. We know their names. How could we not? We love them. I want to help you become part of that second group.

What makes people memorable both offstage and on is their personalities. Successful stand-ups develop memorable personas. As different as one persona is from another, they all share six characteristics. When you achieve these six characteristics you will be a professional stand-up. Here they are:

Originality

Originality is the first and foremost characteristic of a successful stand-up persona. When you are like nobody else, you pop out. How do you achieve originality? The clearest and most concise way I can answer that big question is with this brief story.

I learned how to sail in college. Every week there was a race. I learned basic skills from my instructor and from following the boat that was in the lead. I did pretty well for a new sailor. My boat would finish among the leaders. My instructor complimented me on my growing competency. Then one morning before a race, he asked me, "Rosenfield, do you want to win?" I told him that I'd love to. Then he said, "You'll never come in first by following the boat in front of you."

Achieving an original persona follows the sequence of my sailing education: you learn the basic skills from a book or instructor and from performing as often as possible. You watch and learn and sometimes emulate the stand-ups you most admire. And then, if success is your goal, you take off on a path of your own.

As an example, let's look at the career of a great comedian, Woody Allen. In order to understand his originality as a stand-up, you need some historical context. Before Woody Allen, most stand-ups were married men, and the few female stand-ups were also married. Their jokes were about being married and having a family; their struggles with their spouses, kids, and in-laws; moving from the city to the suburbs; acclimating to suburban life; and so on. Family and married life were also the subjects of most television sitcoms aired at that time—the 1950s: *The Honeymooners, I Love Lucy, I Married Joan, The Danny Thomas Show, The Burns and Allen Show, My Little Margie, The Life of Riley, Father Knows Best, The Adventures of Ozzie and Harriet, Leave It to Beaver.*

And then along came Woody Allen. Not only wasn't he married, he was bitterly divorced, and he did jokes about his ex-wife in his stand-up:

> She was coming home late at night and she was violated—that's how they put it in the New York paper. And they asked if I would comment on it. And I said, "Knowing my wife it probably wasn't a moving violation."
>
> I tended to put my wife under a pedestal.

Allen would move on from these kinds of jokes to jokes about single life:

I want to tell you a terrific story about oral contraception. I asked this girl to sleep with me and she said, "No."

Sex between two people is a beautiful thing; between five it's fantastic.

I read an article in *Life* magazine saying there was a sexual revolution going on on college campuses all over the country, and I reregistered at New York University.

Besides his being divorced and single, another original aspect of Allen's persona was that he was highly neurotic:

I was captain of the latent-paranoid softball team. We used to play all the neurotics on Sunday morning—nail biters against the bed wetters. . . . I used to steal second base, then feel guilty and go back.

I was gonna kill myself, but I was in a strict Freudian analysis and if you kill yourself, they make you pay for the sessions you miss.

Woody Allen broke the 1950s comedy mold. His jokes tapped into the sensibilities of the emerging 1960s generation. It was a generation in rebellion against the '50s way of life: a repressive attitude toward sex, an unthinking acceptance of authority, the bougie suburban life-style, and the overarching aspiration to "fit in." In contrast, Woody Allen's persona was urban, neurotic, horny, and single. Not fitting in to the world of the '50s helped make Woody Allen the comic voice of the '60s generation.

Allen's stand-up and his early movies were about single life in the city. His success with this material led to a sea change in comedy. In the '60s and '70s, suburban family sitcoms found them-selves sharing the airwaves with such shows about urban single life as *That Girl*, *The Mary Tyler Moore Show*, *The Odd Couple*, *Laverne and Shirley*, *Three's Company*, and *Rhoda*. It's a trend that continued

through the '80s right up to the present with shows like *Cheers,
The Golden Girls, Seinfeld, Friends, Girls, New Girl, Broad City,* and
Master of None.

Woody Allen's originality was of epic proportions. His process of
achieving it, however, followed the well-trod path of the successful
stand-ups who came before him and those who would come after
him. He spent about two years performing as often as he could at any
club that would give him stage time. That, along with the mentorship
of his manager, Jack Rollins, enabled him to master the fundamen-
tal techniques of writing and performing stand-up. He also studied
and emulated the comedian he admired the most, Bob Hope. In fact,
Allen has said that his persona was modeled in part on Hope's—the
guy who brags about his success with women until he's actually in
their presence, or even preparing to be, at which time he comically
falls apart. Undergirded by techniques and lessons from role models,
Allen created a persona that was all his own. For instance, unlike
his idol Bob Hope's rapid-fire delivery of one-liners, Allen's delivery
was slower and more conversational. He mixed his one-line observational jokes with longer anecdotal pieces. He was self-deprecating
like Hope, but in an entirely different way. Hope would do jokes
about being a lousy golfer or lover. Allen's self-deprecating jokes were
about being neurotic. Hope dressed and had the look of a big-time
celebrity. Allen looked like an adjunct professor in a college English department whose prospects for tenure weren't good. In fact, if
Woody Allen himself hadn't spoken of emulating Bob Hope, no one
would've noticed it.

You can and should go on this same journey to create an original
persona. It starts with a desire to acquire technique. You can accomplish this by watching skilled comedians at work, reading books, taking comedy classes, and seeking guidance from skilled mentors. The
people who successfully break the rules are people who know them.
You'll hone your skills by performing as often as you can in front of
paying audiences. You'll study the stand-ups you most admire, and
adapt what you learn from them into your own act. And then, you

will eventually stop following the stand-ups in front of you. You will seek a path of your own by listening to *your* sense of humor, *your* imagination, and the laughter of *your* audiences. And please, whatever you do, don't end your set with "That's my time."

Genuineness

The bottom line is the audience has to believe you. If they don't, they won't laugh. That doesn't mean you need to be yourself onstage. You can't be. You're too complicated; we all are. We can spend years with some people and then realize we don't really know them. As a stand-up you don't have years to reveal yourself. You have more like five minutes. So that person onstage is a personality created by the stand-up. It may be close to the stand-up's offstage personality, or it may bear little or no resemblance to it. In either case, the audience has to buy it.

Achieving genuineness starts with your joke writing. What comes out of your mouth doesn't have to be true. It has to *seem* true. So, for instance, when Richard Pryor performed his legendary piece about accidentally setting himself on fire while he was freebasing cocaine, we didn't doubt his story for a second. We knew Richard, so we knew it was true. Only we didn't really know Richard. We knew his persona. And, in fact, it wasn't true. The truth was that it wasn't an accident. It was an attempted suicide. The actual facts, however, don't matter. What matters is his jokes ring true; they are believable. Watching video of his performance, we never think, *Who does this dude think he's kidding? That never happened to him. He's just made up some jokes to get us to laugh. This is bullshit.* What we think is, *He's making us laugh about a near-fatal drug accident. What an amazing comedian!*

What you look like onstage also has to ring true. If Roseanne Barr had made her *Tonight Show* debut wearing the casual, urban, elegant outfits that were popular among her stand-up peers, people would have been utterly confused by her. They would have wondered, *Who the hell is she? Who is she pretending to be?* But that's not what people thought. She wore an out-of-date print jacket and an absurdly large corsage. She started talking in her loud, nasal voice:

> I never get out of the house. I stay home all the time, I never do anything fun, because I'm a housewife. I hate that word, "housewife." I prefer to be called "domestic goddess."

I was watching this on TV and I remember exactly what I said at that point in her set: "Kate [my wife], get in here! You've got to see this!"

Genuineness is an essential attribute of a successful stand-up persona. It's achieved by writing and performing jokes that give the audience the impression that what they're hearing and seeing may be exaggerated but at its core it is the truth. This comedic truth may be created out of real facts or be total figments of your imagination, or both. The bottom line is the audience has to believe it.

Vividness

Steve Allen told me that in 1954, when he first started booking his stand-up buddies on *The Tonight Show*, they would open their sets on TV the same way they did in the clubs in those days: they took their time getting into their jokes. They'd casually ask the audience how they were doing. They would tamp down their cigarette pack, leisurely take out and light a cigarette, do some ad-libbing with Steve, and then after a minute or two had gone by start their act. Steve learned from the Nielsen ratings that during this warm-up time he lost a huge percentage of his audience. If the television audience wasn't engaged by the comedian in the first few seconds of the set, they had an option a club audience didn't have. They could change the channel. So Allen learned to tell his stand-ups to snap right into their routines. Necessity in art is often the mother of excellent things. Television created the need for a stand-up to be a vivid presence within the first few seconds of his or her set. This led to jokes that were much more tightly written and more personal. It also led to stand-ups putting more thought into creating a visual look for themselves that would help establish their personas from the second they walked onstage.

Rodney Dangerfield is a great example of a stand-up who created a vivid persona. At the time of his rise to stardom, the 1960s, there was a uniform for men in comedy: a sports jacket or a suit and tie. Rodney followed this protocol but made it his own. Most stand-ups wanted to look sharp, or at least composed. Not Rodney. He was in a suit and tie, but it looked like he had put on weight and hadn't gone shopping for new clothes. His shirt looked like it didn't quite fit. He'd nervously straighten and restraighten his tie, which sometimes seemed like it was choking him. He looked sweaty. He'd take the stage, look out at the audience with a haunted expression and say, "I get no respect at all." Then he'd follow with his opening jokes:

This one guy gave me a hard time. He kept looking at me and looking at me. Finally he said, "Where do I know you from?" I said, "Do you ever watch *The Tonight Show with Johnny Carson*?" He said, "Yeah, you too?"

I can't relax, you know? The other night I felt like having a few drinks. I went over to the bartender and said, "Surprise me." He showed me a naked picture of my wife.

Last week my house was on fire. My wife told the kids, "Be quiet, you'll wake up Daddy."

I'm so ugly, my father carries around a picture of the kid who came with his wallet.

It took seconds, not minutes, to know exactly who Rodney Dangerfield was.

To achieve this degree of vividness takes time. At the outset of your career you won't yet know exactly who you are onstage. Rodney didn't. He was an unsuccessful stand-up for nine years in the 1940s. He gave it up because he had to make a living to support his family, and spent the next 10 years selling aluminum siding. During his hiatus from comedy he realized that what he lacked as a stand-up was a vivid persona, or "image" as he called it. So in the 1960s he went about creating one. His approach was the time-honored one that you should follow as well: learn to write jokes that, no matter their apparent subjects, ultimately are about you. Don't write generic jokes. If you do, try to sell them to generic stand-ups. Write jokes that no one else could possibly tell as well as you.

Likability

The more the audience likes you, the more they will laugh. If they don't like you, they won't laugh. If they love you, you are on the way to becoming a star. How do you achieve likability? Let me begin by telling you what *not* to do.

Don't feel that you need to be nice. Nice has nothing to do with likability. Larry David in *Curb Your Enthusiasm* is not nice; he's a jerk. He's such a jerk that he gets thrown out of dinner parties, country clubs, and his marriage. When he travels to New York, Mayor Bloomberg throws him out of the city. And yet we love him. The reason why we love him is the key to creating a likable persona.

In each episode of *Curb Your Enthusiasm*, Larry David is positioned in a struggle. Things that might momentarily annoy us drive him crazy for days—weeks even. Larry David's comedy rests on an insight into comedy that Shakespeare gave us in the title of his play *Much Ado About Nothing*. David creates comedies that are much ado about nothing. It's been said that *Seinfeld*, which he cocreated, was about nothing. It wasn't. It was about how the leading characters *got so worked up* over nothing—the dry cleaner's discount coupon, whether or not the "soup Nazi" would serve them soup, or whether the fruit guy would sell them melons. Their struggles are unending, and so is our affection for them.

Take a look at the stand-up jokes in this book. Some seem old-fashioned, others very contemporary; some edgy, some family friendly. But with the exception of some of the put-down jokes, they *all* speak of the stand-up's personal struggles. Lenny Bruce is struggling with the boredom that comes from being on the road. Louis C.K. is struggling with the boredom of playing board games with his young children.

Woody Allen is struggling with his relationships and neuroses. Tig Notaro is struggling with breast cancer. Moms Mabley is struggling with racism and finding a man. Richard Pryor is struggling with his health and racism. Dino Wiand is struggling to fly between two airports in New York City. Eddie Izzard's Darth Vader is struggling to get something to eat in the Death Star cafeteria. Phyllis Diller is struggling with her husband and her looks. Bob Newhart's driving instructor is struggling with a student whose driving is so poor she may kill him. Rodney Dangerfield is struggling with other people's lack of respect for him. Laura Bassi is struggling with being an honors graduate of her university who has to work as a nanny and has no social life. And so on.

You in a personal struggle is the golden land of comedy. Nothing is funnier. Whatever you're talking about in your stand-up, strive to make it personal; make it clear how strongly you feel about it and why it matters to you. And position it so that it's something you're struggling with not in the past but *right now*—this moment onstage. When an audience sees you wrestling with something that really matters to you, they laugh and they love you, because you've just made their own struggles easier to bear.

A good way to see how positioning yourself in a struggle creates likability is to revisit the opening of Chris Rock's put-down jokes about Michael Jackson (see page 43 for the entire quote):

> Michael Jackson lost his mind. What the hell is wrong with Michael? Another kid! Another kid!!!! I thought it was Groundhog's Day when I heard that shit. . . . That's how much we love Michael. We love Michael so much, we let the first kid slide. Another kid! I'm fuckin' done. I'm done with Michael! I'm done, I was a fan my whole life, I am fuckin' done. I'm handing in my glove. OK.

Rock tees up this celebrity put-down piece as his own personal struggle, fueling its comedic firepower with his frustration and anger over having to give up on a beloved star. Rock positioned himself as an adoring fan who had been jilted by his idol. His anger didn't come from malice. It came from a broken heart. That's brilliant comedy writing.

Why does being in a struggle create likability? Consider Rock's routine: Michael Jackson was the biggest pop star of his time. A great many people identified with Rock's struggle to give up his love for Michael. So there's our answer: we like comedians with struggles because we identify with them. All of us, in some ways, are struggling. When stand-ups speak about their struggles, we identify and laugh. And we hear other people laugh. We realize we are not alone in our struggles. We're in this thing together. Together, we can face our struggles and laugh! That's a relief. And that's entertainment!

It's important to realize that having a struggle does not make you a victim. It makes you the leading character in your comedy. It makes you the person the audience is rooting for. And make no mistake, you want the audience to root for you. In tragedy the hero struggles and perishes. To qualify as a comedy, there has to be a happy ending. In comedy the hero is vulnerable, but invincible. He struggles, but he always happily survives and lives on for another day—of more struggles.

You causing a struggle for someone else makes you an unlikable bully. You in a struggle makes you a likable hero.

Stage Presence

Some performers don't engage our full attention. We are able to multitask when they are onstage. We can listen to them and eat or drink or quietly talk among ourselves or to the waitstaff. And then there are those few performers who are so riveting that we can't, even for a moment, take our eyes off them.

These performers have a strong stage presence. I am often asked if a performer can enhance his or her stage presence. The answer is yes.

To understand how this is accomplished, it is important to appreciate one of the underlying reasons why people seek out entertainment. Good entertainment provides us with the opportunity to exercise our feelings. When we are watching a play or a movie or listening to a favorite singer in concert, we can feel joyful or excited, elated or in suspense, melancholy or giddy with laughter. Throughout most of our lives, we occupy places where we have to keep a tight rein on our feelings. At school, at work, and even at home, we often feel the need to hold our feelings in check. Good entertainment enables us to safely drop the reins. It enables us to be moved.

In chapter 26, "Joyous Communication," I describe one of the transformations that occurs when people form an audience. They stop feeling what they're feeling and begin experiencing the feelings that are coming from the performers. If there are no feelings coming from those performers, the audience doesn't feel anything—anything but bored and anxious for the performance to end.

A performer succeeds to the degree that he or she engages the emotions of the audience, moves an audience, provides them with a heightened sense of being alive. The performers who are capable of doing this are the ones who have learned to use their medium to express, in their own way, a vibrant emotional life.

Some performers' emotional lives are writ large—think of stand-ups like Sam Kinison, Lewis Black, Gilbert Gottfried, Chris Rock, Richard Pryor, Joan Rivers, Jessica Kirson, Sebastian Maniscalco, Moms Mabley, Phyllis Diller. Others have a subtle way of conveying how they feel, like Bob Newhart, Tig Notaro, Mitch Hedberg, David Letterman. We in the audience feel alive in the presence of stand-ups who have found their way to comically express their emotional life on stage. Low-energy, deadpan stand-ups who succeed are very much the exception and not the rule.

So an important key to gaining stage presence for a stand-up is to write and perform jokes that convey to your audience how you feel about everything you say. This is the reason I've instructed you to be clear about your attitudes in all of your setups and punchlines.

Being Funny

This may seem self-evident to you. But it's not to a lot of stand-ups. A lot of stand-ups aren't very funny. They're OK. But they're not memorably funny. Are they less talented than their memorable colleagues?

Yes. But in saying yes to this, am I saying that either you're born with it or you aren't? No. And here's why: A lot of what is credited to talent is actually the result of hard work. Studies of people who excel at what they do—whether in the arts, entertainment, sports, science, technology, business, education—have shown that such people have one thing in common: they work harder than their colleagues. Whether it was Tiger Woods showing up days before a match so he could practice a particular shot over and over again, or the dancer and movie star Fred Astaire practicing and refining his steps well after everyone else had gone home for the day, or Jerry Seinfeld working on a joke for several years until he feels he's nailed it. The key ingredient of their excellence isn't talent alone, but talent coupled with hard work.

I'm about to tell you something, and my intention in so doing is not to be inspirational. It's to be realistic and hard headed: You can be as funny as you want to be **if you are prepared to put in the work**, if you refuse to settle for so-so laughs. If your mission is to rock the house and you're willing and eager to put in the necessary work to make it happen, then it will happen, in time. Work hard at it. That's what everyone else who's making it is doing.

36

THE SEVENTH CHARACTERISTIC

WHAT'S YOUR STORY? IF YOU can readily answer that, and you possess the other six characteristics of a successful persona, you may be headed toward stardom.

Major comedians have a characterological narrative—a story that defines the essence of their persona. It has been this way throughout the history of stand-up. Jack Benny's story was that he was a miser. Moms Mabley's story, as she described it herself, was that she was a "dirty old lady" with a penchant for younger men and for telling inconvenient truths about racism. Phyllis Diller was the flamboyant ugly duckling. Woody Allen's story during the period of his stand-up and early movies was about single life in the city. Rodney Dangerfield's story was "I get no respect." Joan Rivers was the no-holds-barred gossip: "Can we talk?" Roseanne Barr was a working-class "domestic goddess." Robin Williams was the hyperkinetic guy bouncing off the walls. Sam Kinison was the rebel warrior reporting back from the front lines of the battle of the sexes, which he was losing, and the battle against political correctness, which he was winning. Jerry Seinfeld is the guy who's bugged by everyday insanities. Amy Schumer is the raunchy feminist. Chelsea Handler is the unapologetic boozer. Louis

C.K. is not a single guy—he's an alone guy. Because of current events, Lewis Black is constantly on the verge of a nervous breakdown. Sarah Silverman is the racist Jewish princess. And so it goes with every star comedian. You may or may not remember their jokes, but you for sure know their stories.

There are also headliners who haven't figured out what their story is. Their acts are funny from beginning to end; audiences enjoy their performances. But something is missing, and its absence is keeping them from rising to the very top. What's missing is their story.

As with all things concerning the creation of a persona, finding your story takes time. You'll find it by writing and performing as much as you can and embracing your audiences as your editor in chief. You'll find it by giving yourself the freedom to follow your imagination and try new things. It's a mistake to settle on a story too soon. It's a mistake, in the beginning of your development, to become conservative, risk averse, afraid of trying something new because you think it might not fit your characterological narrative. If it strikes you as funny, try it. When you do, one of two things will happen. Either it won't work and you'll drop it, or it will work and new possibilities will open up for you—there will be new subjects for you to talk about and added emotional dimensions to your persona.

Some people find their story through a very conscious process. Roseanne Barr has spoken about deciding early on in her career that she wanted to be the female Ralph Kramden—the loudmouthed, lovable bus driver whom Jackie Gleason played in *The Honeymooners*. More often, if you're out there performing, finding your story just happens organically over time; it will crystallize as you discover and focus on the subjects and attitudes that work best for you, and eliminate what doesn't work.

These, then, are the seven characteristics of successful stand-up personas. How long does it take to acquire them? The shortest time I know of for a persona to crystallize is two years. It took Woody Allen that long to create his. But he had several advantages: before he started doing stand-up he had a successful career writing comedy for comedians, including the great Sid Caesar. Then, because of the nature of the stand-up business in those days, and the contacts of his manager, he was able to develop in front of club audiences from the outset. In addition, his manager was an expert in comedy writing and performing. And it didn't hurt that Allen is a comedy genius. Bob Hope said that it took his writers two years to figure out his persona. He felt he had little or nothing to do with it. Most successful comedians say their process took longer. More like four to seven years. The time it takes has nothing to do with a stand-up's eventual success. Stand-ups who take three years developing their personas don't necessarily have more success than stand-ups who take longer. No stand-up was more successful than Steve Martin. At the height of his career, he performed in stadiums in order to accommodate his gigantic fan base. He had to stop performing because his fans were screaming throughout his act and no one could hear a thing. Here is Martin, in his book *Born Standing Up*, on his development timeline:

> I did stand-up comedy for eighteen years. Ten of those years were spent learning, four years were spent refining, and four were spent in wild success.

I know it can be discouraging to think it might take that long to really know what you're doing. But you mustn't be discouraged. Good things, wonderful things, can happen way before a persona fully develops. I've had students signed by agents within the first few months of studying with me. Some of my students, a couple of years out, have made their stand-up debuts on network and premium cable television. It's quite possible to get noticed and get work early on. It takes longer, however, to truly master stand-up comedy—to master the crafts of performing and writing comedy and developing a persona. The fact is, many comedians get work and plateau before their apprenticeship is completed. However, the abiding stars of stand-up complete their comedy education.

There's no such thing as overnight success in stand-up. What a career in stand-up offers is not quick work but a lifetime of work. Don Rickles was busy headlining all the way up to his death at age 90.

37

THE "THIS JOKE USED TO KILL AND NOW IT'S BOMBING, WHAT THE HELL IS GOING ON" CHECKLIST

YOU WILL INEVITABLY ENCOUNTER TIMES when one of your "A" jokes that consistently earned big laughs stops working. Here's a checklist that will help you pinpoint the reason why and tell you what to do about it.

Reason 1

You're not performing it the way you did when it was working. This is the number-one reason that "A" material stops working. It's been months since you created the joke. You've forgotten the attitudes that propelled you to write the joke in the first place and that you played onstage when the joke was still fresh in your gut. You've unintentionally changed the attitudes that made the joke work.

For example, in her single days Mary Dimino had a killer joke about blowing her one chance to get married:

I coulda gotten married. I coulda. If I had just not walked into my engagement party and said, "Wow! There are a lot of great lookin' guys here!"

When Mary wrote this joke, many of her friends were already married and her prospects at the time looked nonexistent. When she performed the setup her attitude was despair. Life had slipped through her fingers. When she delivered the punch—"There's a lot of great looking guys here!"—her attitude flipped from despair to delight. We could see why her fiancé would have called off the marriage. Happily, things changed for Mary. She met a guy and they got engaged. I'd never seen her so happy. Because the joke worked and the audience didn't know that Mary was engaged in her real life, she kept it in her set. It stopped working. I took a look at it in performance and the problem was clear. Mary's off-stage happiness was now coloring the joke. She was beaming with delight when she delivered the setup as well as the punch. It looked like she was thrilled that she would never marry. That new attitude killed the laugh.

Solution: Go back to the attitudes you played when the joke was working. If you have a recording of the performance, review it. When you next perform the joke, play those original attitudes and the laugh will return.

Reason 2

The joke is dated. Sadly, audiences did not have an infinite desire to hear Monica Lewinsky jokes. The George W. Bush jokes were good for eight and a half years, but then, having gone beyond their call of duty, they expired. There were a ton of jokes about the Clinton/Trump presidential election. They won't survive. Given the election results, many of us are wondering whether or not we'll survive. But I digress. If your joke is about something in the news that has already been fodder for talk-show hosts and an uncountable number of other comedians, at some point audiences will have heard all they want to hear on the subject. They communicate this to you by not laughing.

Solution: Cut the joke.

Reason 3

You've moved the placement of a joke, and by so doing you've inadvertently hurt it. There are jokes that appear at first glance to have no relationship with each other. They seem to be standalone jokes that could go anywhere in the set and still score. Sometimes this is in fact the case, and sometimes it's not. It's easy to tell if repositioning the joke has hurt it: the audience stops laughing.

Serkal Kus, a student of mine from Germany, is a comedy writer and stand-up who encountered this situation. Serkal is a charming, intelligent, and likable presence onstage. He has a reliable "A" joke that he placed in the middle of his set:

> This year was crazy, right? Even the Summer Olympics. Americans didn't win gold at shooting.

The joke got such a strong response that he decided to use it as his opening joke. When he did, it tanked. Here's why: This guy comes out onstage with a heavy German accent, says he's from Germany, and the next thing he says to his American audience is that they're so violent they should have won Olympic gold at shooting. It was jarring. He came across to his American audience as opinionated, arrogant, and rude, which Serkal is not. But with this as his first joke, he gave his audience reason to see him that way. Here are some of Serkal's jokes that previously went before the gold joke:

> I'm from Germany. The home of comedy.

> It's weird how at some point in your childhood you learn about this thing called nationality. "I'm German? Ugh." And then my parents said, "Don't worry. Actually, Mommy and Daddy aren't German. We are from the Middle East." (Alarmed) Oh shit!!! Well I guess that explains the chest hair at age six.

> Oh son, one more thing you should know. We are immigrants from Kurdistan, we have no money, and everybody hates us. Have fun at school! "Yallah! Yallah! Yallah!"

Those jokes presented the audience with a totally different picture of Serkal. They're smart and self-deprecating. They position Serkal in a struggle: He's a comedian from a country renowned for having no sense of humor. When he was a child, his disappointment in being German was replaced by fear when he discovered his family isn't German; they are poor emigrants from Kurdistan. Now we're rooting for this guy. We like him. And so when he starts in on his jokes about the US, we think of him not as an arrogant foreigner disparaging our country but as a guy who is grateful to be here, and who is smart enough to realize what's going on in his adopted country. Now we're ready to laugh at the Olympic gold joke.

Solution: If you've moved the joke, put it back where it was: it's not a standalone joke. There's something about its original placement that's essential for it to work. Restore the joke to its original place and the laughs will return, just as they did for Serkal.

Reason 4

The material is inappropriate for a particular audience. I worked with a comic whose set included sexually graphic as well as clean material. He was funny, and eventually he got his first paying gig. He bombed. "Not a single laugh," he told me in the day-after "I BOMBED AND I'M QUITTING THE BUSINESS" phone call. "What material did you do?" I asked. "The dirty stuff," he replied. "Where were you?" I asked. "A bar mitzvah."

Oy.

A group of 13-year-old boys and girls, their parents and grandparents, and a rabbi is not the right audience for dick jokes. Underline that last sentence. Sexually graphic material does not work with children in their early teens; it embarrasses them. At a family gathering where children are present, parents and grandparents will find the material inappropriate. The rabbi will probably not be overjoyed either. Raunchy material works with the late-night, 20s-and-30s, met-the-two-drink-minimum-before-the-show-started, horny-and-single crowd. The older and more sophisticated the crowd, the less they go for sexually explicit jokes.

Solution: Look at the crowd before you go on. See if it's younger or older, and be prepared to change up your set if it looks like the jokes you've selected are wrong for the audience. If you're not up first, listen to the comics who go on before you. If they're getting big laughs with smart, clean material, don't do your roll on "the ten ways your girlfriend passes gas." Save it. Try to hold it in. Thank you. If you're hired to perform during prom week, let 'em rip.

Reason 5

Rosenfield's Law of Relativity. Einstein had his; I have mine. His should be of interest to you if you're concerned about the relative speed of light. Mine should interest you if you're trying to figure out why a good joke has stopped working.

Let's say you've been closing your set with a killer joke that sweeps you offstage to the sounds of laughter, applause, and adulation. Several months later the joke is tanking and you're schlepping offstage to the sounds of cats walking on pillows. You've been through the checklist: you haven't changed the original attitudes, it's not dated or inappropriate to the audience, and you haven't changed its placement. So what's going on? Audiences laugh hardest at what is relatively the funniest material in your set. As you add higher-quality material to your set, what once was a killer joke may now be marginal. That's why the joke is bombing. This is the best reason in the world to cut a joke. You've become a much better writer and your old stuff is not up to your new stuff. Congratulations!

Solution: Cut the joke.

38

HOSTING

IF YOU CAN MC, DO IT. Through no fault of their own, not everyone can. Some stand-ups with eccentric personas can't fill the role of a warm, enthusiastic host. For instance, Stephen Wright is a fine stand-up, but his deadpan delivery would rule him out as an MC. Lewis Black's man-on-the-verge-of-a-nervous-breakdown persona would rule him out as well. In order to host, stand-ups need to have a conversational, cordial, and convivial dimension to their comic personalities. If you possess these qualities, you can and should seek opportunities to host shows. If you get good at it early on in your career, it will open up more gigs for you.

A good MC is an essential component of a good show. Good MCs know how to get an audience laughing right up front. Further, they know how to maintain the laughter and decorum in the room throughout the show. They make the other stand-ups on the bill feel good by giving them gracious and supportive intros and by never getting a laugh at their expense either before or after they perform. Good MCs know to ask the show's producer or club manager what duties they would like the MC to carry out.

The MC occupies a significant role in the evening's proceedings, but he or she is not the star of the show—the headliner is. Neither is the MC the boss—the club manager is. In road gigs, the MC is usually the least experienced stand-up on the bill. However, the MC is the glue that holds the show together. He or she is the facilitator of a smoothly running, entertaining show.

The most successful MC in the history of American show business was Ed Sullivan. He had no act; all he did was host. He'd greet the audience at the beginning of his television show, and at the end he'd thank them and wish them good night. In-between, he'd introduce the acts.

He was awkward looking. His shoulders were hiked up to his ears. His gestures were big and broad and often seemed to have nothing to do with what he was saying. He managed, somehow, to have both a forceful and mumbling delivery, so you could clearly hear him and still not know what he was saying. He was a favorite of impressionists for decades. Yet *The Ed Sullivan Show* was must-see-TV on a scale that has never been equaled. His success as a television personality clearly had nothing to do with comedy talent or charisma. It had to do with something else—enthusiasm.

Ed Sullivan greeted his audience every Sunday night at 8:00 PM with the promise that they were about to see "a really big show." He mispronounced the word *show* so it sounded more like *shoe*. Nonetheless, his vast audience got the message. He introduced every act, whether it was the Beatles or the juggler who spun plates on top of poles, with unbridled enthusiasm. Each show ended with the promise that another great "shoe" was in store for next Sunday.

The key to MCing, revealed to us by Mr. Sullivan, is to be enthusiastic. Be enthusiastic about everything—the show, the club, the waitstaff, the audience, and the acts. Remember, the audience feels what the performer feels. An MC who lacks enthusiasm will bring the audience down even if the stand-ups are funny. An MC who is sarcastic, who tries to get laughs at the expense of the club or the audience or the other comedians, creates resentment and a sour mood.

Here is a step-by-step guide to hosting:

The MC Set

Your MC set cannot simply be your usual set. It needs to meet certain requirements that apply only to the host's set. First off, it should be clean. The audience is just settling in and getting to know you. It is too early for raunchy material, edgy material, or the big curse words. Part of your job as MC is to make the audience feel comfortable and certain that they will be in good hands throughout the show. By working clean and funny, you give everyone in the audience that assurance.

It's best not to do long, anecdotal pieces as an MC. The distractions of the waitstaff taking orders and delivering the first round of drinks makes it difficult for an audience to pay the kind of close attention an extended anecdotal piece requires.

It's good to have short observational jokes. If something newsworthy has recently occurred, and it's not tragic or sad, it's good to have jokes about it. In this regard, the late-night talk show monologues are models of how to successfully open a show. Observational jokes about yourself are fine too, as long as they're not dark or edgy. Crowd work, if it is written and tried and true, is a good way to engage individual audience members and get them focused on the stage.

It's not a good idea to try out new material or do much ad-libbing if you're hosting. A big part of your job is to get the audience laughing. You are most likely to accomplish this with clean, short, tried-and-true jokes.

Before the Show Starts

Get to the club early so you can take care of your preshow responsibilities. If you haven't already done so, find out if there are announcements the show's producer or club manager wants you to make. You want to give yourself time to familiarize yourself with these announcements. If possible, you don't want to refer to notes when you deliver them. You want them to sound like they're coming from you. Think of the announcements as a commercial you've been hired to perform, and deliver them with conviction and enthusiasm. You don't want to sound like you're announcing the license plate number of a car that needs to be moved. Also, find out if there's anything the manager *doesn't* want you to say. Some clubs, for instance, don't want their MCs to mention other clubs by name in the performers' intros.

When the other stand-ups arrive, find out how they want to be introduced. Part of your job is to assure them the show will be in good hands and you'll be working to make them look good. Make sure you're certain how to properly pronounce their names. Mispronouncing stand-ups' names when you introduce them will throw them off right at the top of their sets. It forces them to deal with correcting your error, rather than starting with their planned opening jokes. It rightfully pisses them off. Also, ask them if they have any credits they'd like you to mention in your introduction. Once they've given you that information, say it back to them to make sure you have it right and they're comfortable with what you're going to say.

In addition to getting their names and credits right, you want to say something positive about them. If you like their work, say so in your introduction: "I love this guy's comedy and I know you will too." If you're unfamiliar with their work, say something like, "I know you're going to enjoy our next performer." If they've never performed before, say something like, "This is exciting. Our next performer is making her stand-up comedy debut for you tonight. Let's give her a really warm welcome." Saying something positive will get the audience excited about who's up next; equally important, it makes the stand-up you're introducing feel confident.

There are several things you do *not* want to do in an introduction. You don't want to oversell the performer by saying something like "There's nobody funnier than our next performer . . ." That kind of over-the-top introduction angers stand-ups, because it puts them under undue pressure. Also, you never *ever* want to get a laugh at the expense of a stand-up you're introducing. Doing so is a mortal sin. You don't want to say something like "Our next performer has been on Jimmy Fallon. Not the show. She's just been on Jimmy Fallon." Something like this may or may not get a laugh from the audience. But it's guaranteed to make the stand-up furious at you and give you a bad reputation in the comedy community.

If there are debuting comedians in the lineup, an encouraging word from you before the show will help their confidence. The most important thing you can say to them is to have fun and enjoy talking to the audience. Don't tease them by saying scary or negative things. "You better be funny tonight" is the last thing a new or, for that matter, a seasoned stand-up needs to hear before she goes on. Ask the producer how much time each comedian gets and whether you should let the stand-ups know. Also ask the producer whether he'll be timing the acts or wants you to do it. Be certain that you know the signal system for communicating with the stand-ups when they're approaching their allotted time. As explained in chapter 31, it's usually a red light. Traditionally, a flashing red light means wrap it up and a solid light means stop. Ask the producer if you should convey this information to the stand-ups. Part of your job is getting the show in on time. It's also important to know how much time *you* have been allotted, and whether that time includes or excludes your announcements.

Usually the MC is introduced by the club manager on an offstage mic. Write out what you want the manager to say about you. If your name can be easily mispronounced, go over it with the manager. He wants to get your name right.

It's also helpful to ask the waitstaff if they need you to tell them when there's about 20 minutes left in the show. This gives them sufficient time to get the last round of drinks on the tables and drop the checks.

By making these preparations before the show starts, you'll help ensure a smoothly running show and a positive preshow vibe among the performers and waitstaff.

Showtime

Hit the stage with energy and enthusiasm. Remember, they feel what you feel. Warmly greet the audience. It can be useful up front to take a gauge of the audience's level of enthusiasm by asking something like, "Are you ready for a great show?!" If you get a big, enthusiastic response, compliment the audience: "Wow! You guys are a fantastic audience! This is going to be fun!" If their response isn't enthusiastic, pump them up by saying something like, "Oh, I know you can do better than that. We're all here together, your drinks are delicious, the stand-ups are hilarious, so let me hear you: Are you ready for a great show?!!" Then compliment them for their more enthusiastic response. Part of your job is generating and maintaining the audience's enthusiasm throughout the show.

In the event the audience is small, don't draw attention to it. A small audience may be disappointing to you, but not to them. They are there to have fun. Don't bring them down.

Make your announcements, do your set. Sometimes an unresponsive, "cold" crowd is resistant to hearing comedy material right away. In these cases, it's good to just talk to them a bit before going into your jokes. Talk to them about uncontroversial, everyday things they know about—the weather, the traffic, celebrity news. If possible, chat about something that can lead you gracefully into your first joke. When you sense they've settled down and are listening, start your set. Finish your set on time. As the host, you may be the timekeeper. If that's the case, there won't be anyone to signal you that you've gone over your time. To ensure that you're on target, carefully time your set beforehand.

The worst MC I've ever seen was determined to end her set with a big laugh. She didn't get one, so she kept going. And going. And still no big laugh, and on she went. The show's producer signaled her to stop by turning on the red stop light. She ignored it. Finally, in desperation, the producer walked toward the stage. She saw him and stopped. Because of her, the show got off to a terrible start. She not only freaked out the producer, she freaked out the first performer who watched the host eat up some of his stage time. As you'll see in a moment, this host from hell was not done sabotaging the evening's festivities.

When you finish your set and the announcements, introduce the first performer. Here's another intro mistake to avoid: If you are familiar with a stand-up's jokes, do not say anything to reference them. If, for instance, you know a comedian has jokes about his or her parents, don't say anything like, "If you think your parents are weird, wait till you hear what our next comic has to say about hers."

Don't give away anything that has to do with a stand-up's material. You may very well throw off their laughs by doing so.

The order of an introduction generally goes like this:

1. The performer's credits: "Our next performer appears in clubs all over town and can be seen next Thursday night on *Gotham Live* . . ."
2. Something nice: "Please welcome a very funny guy . . ."
3. Their name: "Mike Jones!"

If you've been hand-holding the mic during your set, move the microphone and stand back to center stage before you start your introduction. You don't want the next stand-up to waste precious stage time putting the mic and mic stand back where they belong. The host from hell was all the way stage right when she saw the producer heading toward her. From there, she introduced the first stand-up and handed him the microphone stage right. This stand-up worked with the microphone in the stand, which the host had left all the way on the other side of the stage. This show was a competition held on the large main stage at Gotham Comedy Club. Each performer was given three and a half minutes. So this performer had to eat up his stage time walking from one end of the stage to the other to get the stand, and then walking to center stage to get in position. In the meantime, his entrance applause had died out. There was a good 5 or 10 seconds of dead, awkward silence before he got the mic in place and could start his first joke. He was understandably rattled when he began. He is a pro, so he recovered. But there was no question that the opening moments of his act were undermined by the host's ineptitude.

There is simple choreography involved in turning the stage over to the next comedian. First of all, you never want to have an empty stage. If no one is onstage, there isn't any reason for the audience to applaud. Therefore you want to remain onstage until the next performer arrives. At the end of your introduction, here are the moves to make:

1. Lead the applause for the next performer.
2. Make eye contact with the performer as he or she is entering. If you applaud and look away from the entering performer, you give the impression that you are bored out of your tree.
3. Step away from the microphone so the entering performer has a clear path to the mic.
4. Greet the performer. You are the host. It's your party. Greet your guest. But make your greeting silent: a handshake, a fist bump, a tap on the shoulder. And make it brief; you don't want the entrance applause to die out while you're still onstage.
5. Exit.

Because you don't want an empty stage, be in position to quickly get back onstage when each stand-up finishes. If the stand-up is still dealing with putting the mic and stand back in place, finish the job for him so he can make his exit while there is still applause. Pump up the exit applause by repeating the stand-up's name, saying something like "Mike Jones! Let him hear you!" If he crushed, acknowledge it: "That was awesome! Mike Jones! Let him hear you!"

But if the stand-up tanked, then what?

You don't want to say someone was terrific when he or she wasn't. You need to maintain your credibility with the audience. You also don't want to bring attention to the fact that a stand-up has bombed. Neither the stand-up nor the audience appreciates it when a host makes a snarky remark about a poor performance. What you do in this case is first pump up the exit applause by repeating the stand-up's name. Then briefly do a few of your tried-and-true jokes to get the audience laughing again. Don't go on too long. Remember, you want to bring the show in on time. A good MC never brings a performer to the stage when the audience is dead or inattentive. Never. If people in the audience are talking, quiet them down. Do it in a friendly and humorous way, saying something like, "Hey guys, I need your attention up here. Don't leave me now!" If that doesn't work, just tell them nicely to be quiet. It's part of your job to maintain both laughter and decorum throughout the show. Most nights, that's easy; some nights it's less so. Get good at it and gigs will come your way.

When you're hosting, you have responsibilities to carry out between acts, so stay in the club room during the show. You may be responsible for timing the acts and giving the wrap-up and stop signals. Also, a stand-up may end sooner than expected, in which case you need to hop back onstage and introduce the next act. It would be disastrous for you to be outside the club room having a smoke or chatting if this were to occur. Don't drink alcohol when you're off-stage: you need to be at the top of your game throughout the show. To do your job, you need to be focused on the whole show, not just your time onstage. With a clear mind, watching the other stand-ups perform will give you time to think of something appropriate to say when you're leading the exit applause. Also, it is a red flag for the club to see its host drinking. It is alarming for a club manager to see anyone on duty drinking. The MC is not an exception. Although you're neither the headliner nor the boss, when you host a show, it's your show. To take good care of it, to make it rock, you need to be in the club room, alert, sober, and ready to rumble.

Somewhere near the end of the show lead a round of applause for the waitstaff, and encourage the audience to generously tip them. They'll appreciate you for doing this and they will have earned your praise. Taking and delivering orders, dropping checks, and collecting payment quietly and unobtrusively so as not to disturb the performance is a skill deserving a round of applause.

At the end of the show, lead another round of applause, this time for all the performers. If there are end-of-show announcements, deliver them with conviction. Finish up by thanking the audience warmly and wishing them good night.

39

THE VOICE

IF YOU ARE THINKING NEGATIVE thoughts about your work and these thoughts are making you feel anxious, frightened, unworthy of pursuing your dream, inferior to your colleagues, and ready to quit—you are suffering from *the voice*. This is a common occurrence, and there's no reason for alarm. I'm going to teach you how to successfully cope with it. It's important that you address this condition early on. Left unchecked, *the voice* will, at the very least, hobble your career, and at worst it could destroy it. But we're not going to let that happen.

There's an important distinction to make between *the voice* and nerves. Nerves are a healthy, helpful response to knowing you're about to perform. We experience nerves as heightened excitement. It's like the feelings some people experience before they get on a roller coaster. Thoughts caused by nerves run like this:

Oh my God, I'm really going to do this. I hope I remember my lines. Do I have my cheat sheet? OK. Take a deep breath. Wait a minute, is Michael here yet? He's always late. He can't be late to this. That's my intro! Wake me up when it's over!

Nerves feel exciting and fun scary, roller coaster scary. *The voice* is not fun scary. It's terrifying. *The voice* doesn't help you the way your nerves do. Its intent is to hurt you. Its intent is to stop you from doing what you feel you've been put on this Earth to do. Usually, the more you perform the less nervous you feel. You stop worrying about knowing your lines. You have experience handling all sorts of audiences—large, small, generous, cold. The intensity of *the voice*, however, never diminishes, unless you know how to silence it. I'm going to teach you how to do that right now.

The first step in silencing *the voice* is to understand what it really is. What makes it dangerous to your career is that it disguises its true identity. It presents itself to you as accurate, highly critical, anxiety-provoking thoughts about your comedy writing and performing and about your relationships with your peers and mentors. When you're in the grip of *the voice*, you think thoughts like these:

> *I'm not funny. No one is laughing at my jokes. If some people are laughing it's because they feel sorry for me. The other stand-ups are way funnier than me. I don't belong here. The people telling me I'm funny are lying to me. I'm making a fool of myself. I should quit.*

That is *the voice*'s disguise. It pretends to be an accurate, fair critic speaking to you about the work you're doing now. But it's not. In reality it's an old, frightening parental voice from your past. In our childhoods, no one could scare us as much as our parents could. Even the best-intentioned parents on occasion scare the bejesus out of their children. And depending on the degree that parents instill fear, that fear is retained into adulthood.

The voice is a voice from the past. It has a very specific mission. **Its aim is to make you give up on what you want to do the most, and what, in your heart of hearts, *you know you can do*. It wants you instead to abandon your adult aspirations and move back in with Mom and Dad**, literally if they are still with us and figuratively if they have departed. You will not hear a peep from *the voice* if you're entertaining a pipe dream—a dream that you know is a complete fantasy that can't possibly come true. For instance, I love basketball. I love to play it; I love to watch it on TV. When I daydream about giving up what I'm doing now and becoming a professional basketball player, I don't have a single anxiety-producing, negative thought about it. That's because I know there isn't a snowball's chance in Trump National Golf Club Mar-a-Lago that it could actually happen.

But I've had personal experience with *the voice*. It was not connected to performing. It was connected to an important business decision I needed to make. The American Comedy Institute was located in a small office that we'd outgrown because of the increase in our student population and staff. In addition, our landlord announced that the building was about to be torn down. So it was time to move to a new and larger space. I found a perfect place. It was better located for our students and staff. It was large enough for us to stay put and continue to grow. The price was right. I loved it. That's when *the voice* kicked in. I was walking over to the new space to sign the lease when I was hit by a wave of anxiety. This is what went through my mind:

Signing that lease will be a catastrophic mistake. You can't afford the rent. You can't stay in your old office either. You're trapped. You're going out of business. Pathetic.

These thoughts frightened me despite the fact that:

1. Business was better than ever; that's why I needed to move.
2. The new office space was so large that I could hold classes there as well as have plenty of room for me and the staff. This meant I would no longer have to pay rent on both an office space and a studio space. We would actually save on operating costs.
3. I loved the place, and so did the staff and students whom I asked to check it out before I decided to sign the lease.

As a married middle-aged man with two children and a mortgage, the daydream of starting a new career in professional basketball produced in me nary a negative thought. But as a successful producer and teacher of comedy, I was wracked with anxiety about moving into a wonderful and economically sensible new location.

The picture of me painted by *the voice* was the portrait of a failure. That is the picture *the voice* wants you to have of yourself. It is not threatened by your pipe dreams because it knows you will never act on them. It is not threatened by your setbacks, because they contribute to that negative picture. *The voice* is threatened by your success; it's threatened by you moving forward on the path that you know is the right path for you. It fails if you succeed. If you succeed, you won't move back in with your parents. You'll have a place and a life of your own. The more you succeed, the louder *the voice* becomes. It is a reason that some people, on the cusp of success, self-sabotage. When you are in its grip, *the voice* convinces you to believe dreadful thoughts about yourself that others close to you would find utterly absurd.

There are three steps to take that will release you from *the voice*'s grip:

1. Identify *the voice*. It's easy to do. If you're thinking negative things about your work that make you feel anxious, afraid, and inferior, and make you want to give up, that is *the voice*. The coupling of negative thoughts and anxiety is the tip-off.

Consider this: You possess actual, legitimate critical faculties that help you improve your work. These faculties guide you in deciding where your material needs editing, what to keep, what to rewrite, what to chuck, where to adjust an attitude. These faculties give you ideas and thoughts that improve your work, not ones that scare you and make you want to give up. When you work to strengthen your act, it makes you feel creative, not afraid. It's the feeling of anxiety that signals the presence of *the voice*.

By identifying *the voice*, you are identifying the real source of your anxiety. It is not your work. It is not about this show, this audience, this piece of material. It is not about *now*. The source of your anxiety is a voice from the distant past. This voice is an expert at scaring you.

However, it knows absolutely nothing about comedy—which brings us to step 2.

2. Shut it off—because thankfully, *the voice* is always wrong. I say "thankfully" because if this weren't the case, if, like a stopped clock, it were randomly and occasionally correct, it would be well-nigh impossible to differentiate it from the legitimate criticism of your work. Happily, this is not the case. In this world of ours, where every day is filled with uncertainties, one thing you can absolutely count on is that *the voice* is wrong.

I witness this over and over again in my work with performers. An actor will be accomplishing breakthrough work in a rehearsal I'm directing. Her colleagues and I will be watching her in awe when suddenly she stops and says she can't continue the scene because her work is false, phony, a lie, shit. Or I want to review a video of a stand-up's performance, and he begs me not to put it on because he thinks it was a total bomb. I insist, and when his performance appears onscreen there are big laughs from the first joke on. *The voice* has completely distorted these performers' view of their work.

This makes sense in light of *the voice*'s mission: to make you give up on what you know you can do and what you want to do more than anything else.

The voice is wrong. Don't buy into it; don't have a beer with it; don't go for a walk with it; don't listen to it. What it is saying is worthless. Tell it to SHUT UP and move on . . .

3. Turn *the voice*'s negative message into a positive one—because *the voice* is not simply wrong, it is *exactly* wrong. The truth is always the exact opposite of what *the voice* is telling you. So if you want to know your legitimate feeling and thoughts about your work, take *the voice*'s negative message and say it back to yourself *positively*. Say, for example, that you're in a comedy workshop and you're watching the stand-ups who are performing before you. If you start feeling panicky because you're thinking about how unfunny you are, and how if you don't do the sensible thing and split you will humiliate yourself—that means, deep down, you are thinking:

Some of these people are really funny and so am I. I was nervous about taking this workshop, but I faced my fears and now I'm here. And I see now that I should be here! I'm finally where I belong!

That's what you *really* think and feel. *The voice* is a backhanded compliment and a sign of progress. You hear it only when you're succeeding and feeling good about your work. You are entitled to those positive feelings and thoughts. You've earned them. They are yours. Don't let *the voice* take them away.

My experience is that most people in the arts and entertainment will encounter *the voice* at some point, to some degree. It's kind of like catching a cold. It's common; it comes and goes throughout your life. If you take care of it, it can't hurt you. If you don't take care of it, it can turn into something serious.

Again, here are three steps to take when *the voice* starts rattling you:

1. Identify it.
2. Remember it's wrong and shut it off.
3. Restate its negative message to yourself in positive terms, and embrace your progress and success.

Knowing this will transform *the voice* from a potent, malignant cancer on your career to a little sneeze.

God bless you.

40

EVERYTHING YOU NEED TO KNOW ABOUT THE BUSINESS OF STAND-UP COMEDY

BUSINESS IS GOOD. Don't go back to the copyright page to see what year I wrote this rosy business report to see if it still applies. The year doesn't matter. For skilled comedians, business is always good. It's the business of *presenting* stand-up that changes. Stand-ups first appeared in vaudeville shows, which presented a variety of acts—singers, dancers, acrobats, magicians. Then vaudeville died. It was replaced by nightclubs. The acts, including stand-ups, moved to this new venue. Stand-ups also moved into a powerful new entertainment platform—radio. Then radio died and comedians moved to a newer entertainment platform—television. Then nightclubs died and were replaced by folk-music and jazz clubs, which also featured stand-ups. The popularity of these clubs ebbed and a new kind of club came into being—the comedy club. Now television is fading, the digital world is booming, and stand-ups are at the forefront of this new entertainment format.

And so it goes. Adapting to new venues is relatively easy for stand-ups. They don't have to invent new ways of performing; they stand and they talk. If there's a new venue, just show them where to stand and they're in business.

In the past, the sage business advice to new comedians was get good, get seen, get paid. This advice no longer holds.

When comedy clubs first opened in the 1960s and '70s, getting paid was not an issue for new comedians because none of the stand-ups got paid. The fact that you didn't have to pay the talent was a reason that drew some entrepreneurs into opening comedy clubs. By the end of the '70s and into the '80s, comedy clubs became a big and profitable business, and owners could no longer justify requiring stand-ups to work for free. It was still a rough-and-tumble business in those days. Promises of getting paid, and actually getting paid, were often two different things. The advice to performers in those days was don't leave the club until you get your money. The business environment in most clubs is considerably more civilized now. Bookers are up front about the pay, and although it's always a good idea to be vigilant about getting your money, it is the rule and not the exception that you will be paid in a timely fashion. So getting paid, for all intents and purposes, is no longer an issue. If you get booked, you'll get paid.

Before the advent of the Internet, it was a challenge to get seen by club bookers. That's no longer the case. Virtually all club bookers, even those at the most prestigious comedy clubs, will look at a video sent to them by an unknown stand-up. The question isn't whether or not they will look at your video; the question is how long will they look at your video. Will they look at it for 30 seconds, determine that you're not good enough to play their club, and stop watching? Or will they love what they're seeing, watch the whole video, and book you? (The video should be 5 to 10 minutes long. It shouldn't be excerpts of your best performances; it should be one performance. Bookers want to see that you can sustain a performance.) The one and only part of the old show business adage that still stands is: **get good, get undeniably good**. The only people who make it in stand-up have put in the time and work required to accomplish this.

Of course it always helps to know people in the business. They can open a door for you. But then what?

Taking advantage of connections in stand-up comedy is like taking advantage of connections in bullfighting. Let's say you want to be a bullfighter. You've read a book about bullfighting and you've practiced the matador moves on a local calf. Your uncle is good friends with the guy who owns the bullfighting ring and prevails upon him to give you a shot in the big arena. The day comes. You're announced, the crowd cheers; now there's just one problem: There is an enormous friggin bull coming at you! Mommy!!

Whether you aspire to be a bullfighter or a comedian, there is no skipping over the work required to get undeniably good. Then and only then will you get paid to do stand-up. And be assured that when this happens, when you are consistently getting strong laughs throughout your set, night after night, in big clubs and small clubs, in front of hometown audiences and audiences of strangers, you will join the ranks of the pros. Just as there are no overnight successes in stand-up comedy, there are no undiscovered great comedians. When you get big laughs, people in the business notice.

The ballgame is to get good. This is accomplished through training, performing, writing, and persevering.

Training

Training under the guidance of a gifted stand-up teacher will speed up your development, and fortify your decision to pursue standup as a career. On page 120 I give you a guideline to determine whether or not a stand-up teacher is right for you. In designing your overall course of study as a comedian, I urge you to fearlessly determine where you want your comedy to take you and get the training that will enable you to successfully compete in those areas.

Stand-ups regularly enjoy careers as actors, writers, producers, and directors. Think big about the places you want to go with your comedy. Do it now, so you can get the training and education you need to work in those places. If you want to be an actor, take acting classes. If you want to write, educate yourself in comedy writing. Study the movie, television, and theater comedies you admire and use what you learn from your observations to write your own material for these mediums. Read books about comedy writing; take courses on comedy writing. Find and create opportunities for your writing to be performed. The only way you can know for sure if what you've written is funny is to perform it for an audience.

Performing

Perform as often as you can, anywhere and anytime you can. The techniques you learn from good stand-up comedy books and classes can significantly speed up your development. Applying what you've learned over and over again in performance will deepen, expand, and advance your stand-up capabilities. Use every opportunity your local clubs offer to get stage time. Apply to perform at comedy festivals. Seek out storytelling and poetry venues that also welcome comedians. Get the word out that you're doing stand-up. Look for opportunities to perform in events sponsored by organizations you belong to—school, church, and charity fundraisers, high school and college reunions, etc. Here is one good way to measure what it takes to become a professional standup: 1,000 performances.

Writing

In addition to writing and performing your stand-up, look around for outlets for other comedy writing opportunities: a local newspaper, magazines, websites. Write a comedy blog; use social media as an outlet for your comedy. Create a portfolio of your best written and videoed comedy writing so when opportunities present themselves, you have evidence of your skill.

Persevering

To master stand-up comedy you have to persevere. It takes years to get good at it. The best advice I've ever heard on perseverance came from Eddie Murphy. He said that he never gave himself a year or two or any time limit to make it. He decided that he was going to be the best comedian he could be. Having made this decision, he kept moving forward toward his goal and never looked back. Great advice.

Success in any endeavor ultimately comes down to how hard you work at maximizing the gifts you were born with and the skills that you've learned. It's not where you start; it's where you finish. I have seen, on many occasions, new stand-ups who came blazingly out of the gate go nowhere, as well as new stand-ups who seemed to be headed at alarming speed to a rendezvous with their "plan B" become national headliners. The difference is that some people have the will and capacity to work hard and continually improve at what they do, and others don't. The ball is in your court.

When you do the work I'm urging you to do and doors of opportunity open for you, you will enter them with the confidence of knowing *I can do this.*

People need comedy. We know this because comedy has been around forever, everywhere. Persevere, work hard, and get undeniably good and you will work in comedy clubs and theaters, on radio and television, in the movies, in the print and digital world, and whatever is coming next.

Let me know if you have any questions. You can reach me at Stephen@StephenRosenfieldComedy.com.

ACKNOWLEDGMENTS

Special thanks to:

Kirsten Lagatree, who gave me the push I needed and the guidance to write my book proposal.

Julie Schoerke, who got me to the perfect agent for my book.

My agent and editor, Barbara Braun

My editors at Chicago Review Press, Yuval Taylor and Devon Freeny.

Laura Bassi, whose work as a contributor, editor, and researcher was a steadfast source of strength and wisdom for me from the first day to the last day of writing this book.

My in-the-trenches day-to-day editors Kate Redway and Nathaniel Rosenfield.

The comedians and comedy writers whose works I have drawn on to illustrate the process of mastering stand-up comedy: Myron Cohen, Jay Leno, Johnny Carson, Lenny Bruce, George Carlin, Richard Pryor, Jackie "Moms" Mabley (Loretta Mary Aiken), Jerry Seinfeld, Tig Notaro, Mark Twain, Hannibal Buress, Dino Wiand, Eddie Izzard, Bob Newhart, Louis C.K., Marina Franklin, David Letterman, Conan O'Brien, George Lopez, Craig Ferguson, Stephen Colbert, Chris Rock, Rodney Dangerfield, Phyllis Diller, T. J. Miller, Ricky Gervais, Don Rickles, Lisa Lampanelli, Jackie Mason, Clayton Fletcher, Laura

Bassi, Moshe Kasher, Mary Dimino, Joan Keiter, Sarah Silverman, Kate Redway, Steve Martin, Gilbert Gottfried, Paul Reubens, Andy Kaufman, Will Rogers, Bob Hope, Sam Kinison, Molière, "Weird Al" Yankovic, Rich Little, George Burns and Gracie Allen, Jeff Dunham, Terry Fator, Jonathan Winters, Woody Allen, Olga Namer, Jim Gaffigan, Rock Albers, Henny Youngman, Rosco Nash, Aise O'Neil, Steven Wright, Jimmy Fallon, Groucho Marx, Roseanne Barr, Serkal Kus.

Sean Flynn, for his input on the "Hosting" chapter, and for being the best club manager I've ever encountered.

Chris Mazzilli, for giving my students the opportunity to develop at his great club, Gotham Comedy Club.

Lexi Cullen-Baker, whose help in all things is invaluable to me.

Judd Jones, for his encouragement and insights.

Eli Krupnick, who got all of this started.

My students, who have made my work a joy.

Kate, Ben, and Nate, whose steadfast love and encouragement make everything possible.

INDEX

ABOUT THE AUTHOR

Stephen Rosenfield is the founding director of the American Comedy Institute. He coaches and directs stand-ups and actors ranging from beginners to Oscar-nominated talent and winners of MAC, Obie, Emmy, and Tony awards. His stand-up students' accomplishments include performing in the top clubs in North America and around the world; creating and starring in their own sitcoms on HBO, Comedy Central, and TV Land; and starring in stand-up comedy specials on Netflix and Comedy Central. They've appeared on every late-night TV talk show and are the hosts of talk shows on Televisa and Fox Networks. They are published authors, and their comedy writing credits include *Saturday Night Live*, *The Daily Show*, *Full Frontal with Samantha Bee*, *Girls*, *Late Night with David Letterman*, and *The Jim Gaffigan Show*. As actors, they've appeared on Broadway, in network and premium cable television series, and in major motion pictures.

Stephen has been a guest artist and lecturer in comedy at the University of Florida, Brigham Young University, Virginia Commonwealth University, Barnard College, the University of Washington, the New School, New York University, Lawrence University, and the Union Theological Seminary. He was the founding artistic director of Humber College's comedy program, a professor of theater and comedy, and the director of the comedy program at William Paterson

University. He is currently on the board of directors of the National Association of Schools of Theatre (NAST). Stephen has a BA in theater and drama cum laude from Lawrence University and an MFA in theater direction from Stanford University.

The *New York Times* called Stephen "the best known comedy teacher in the country."